UNLOCKING THE MYSTERIES OF

DANIEL

A Comprehensive Study of Prophetic Symbols and Their Meaning

Dr. Maxwell Shimba

Shimba Publishing, LLC.

Printed in the United States of America

TABLE OF CONTENTS

INTRODUCTION

The Book of Daniel stands as one of the most profound prophetic books in the Bible, rich with symbols and visions that have intrigued scholars and believers for centuries. This book seeks to delve into these symbols, exploring their meanings and implications for both the ancient world and contemporary times. Through a meticulous analysis of Daniel's visions and their interpretations, we aim to uncover the deeper truths embedded in these prophetic symbols.

The Historical and Cultural Context

Understanding the historical and cultural backdrop of the Book of Daniel is essential to grasp its profound symbolism. Written during a time of great turmoil and upheaval for the Jewish people, Daniel's prophecies emerge from the context of the Babylonian exile. The Babylonian conquest of Judah and the subsequent exile of the Jewish people marked a period of intense suffering and existential crisis. In this foreign land, Daniel and his companions were forced to navigate the complexities of maintaining their faith and identity amidst a dominant pagan culture.

The Structure and Content of Daniel

The Book of Daniel is divided into two main sections: historical narratives (chapters 1-6) and apocalyptic visions (chapters 7-12). The historical narratives provide a backdrop that sets the stage for the apocalyptic visions, illustrating the faithfulness of Daniel and his companions in the face of immense challenges. These narratives are not merely historical accounts but are imbued with symbolic meaning, demonstrating God's sovereignty and the power of faith.

The apocalyptic visions, on the other hand, plunge into a series of symbolic and often enigmatic images. These visions include the famous accounts of the four beasts, the ram and the goat, the seventy weeks, and the kings of the North and South. Each vision is laden with symbols that speak to the unfolding of divine history and the ultimate triumph of God's kingdom.

The Importance of Symbolism

Symbols play a crucial role in the Book of Daniel, serving as vehicles for conveying deep spiritual truths. Unlike straightforward historical or doctrinal writings, the symbolic nature of Daniel's visions invites readers into a realm where meanings are multi-layered and often require careful interpretation. These symbols are not arbitrary; they are deeply rooted in the cultural, religious, and political milieu of the time. For instance, the imagery of beasts and horns draws from ancient Near Eastern iconography and conveys specific messages about power, dominion, and divine intervention.

Interpreting Prophetic Symbols

Interpreting the prophetic symbols in Daniel requires a multi-faceted approach. Historical-critical methods help us understand the immediate context and original audience of the text. Theological analysis allows us to explore the broader spiritual implications of the visions. Additionally, typological and eschatological readings provide insights into how these symbols foreshadow future events and the ultimate fulfillment of God's redemptive plan.

Relevance for Contemporary Times

While the Book of Daniel was written in a specific historical context, its messages resonate profoundly with contemporary readers. The themes of faithfulness in adversity, the sovereignty of God, and the hope of ultimate deliverance are timeless. In a world that continues to grapple with political upheaval, moral crises, and existential uncertainties, Daniel's visions offer a source of encouragement and a reminder of the enduring nature of God's promises.

Objectives of This Book

This book aims to provide a comprehensive exploration of the prophetic symbols in the Book of Daniel. By examining each vision in detail, we will uncover the historical context, symbolic meanings, and theological implications. Our goal is to offer readers a deeper understanding of Daniel's prophecies and to illuminate how these ancient symbols speak to our lives today.

Through careful analysis and thoughtful interpretation, we hope to shed light on the mysteries of the Book of Daniel and inspire a renewed appreciation for its profound insights. Whether you are a scholar, a student of the Bible, or a curious reader seeking to understand the prophetic literature, this book endeavors to be a valuable resource in your journey.

A Journey of Discovery

As we embark on this journey of discovery, it is important to approach the Book of Daniel with both reverence and curiosity. The rich tapestry of symbols woven throughout Daniel's visions invites us to explore the depths of God's revelation. By delving into the historical background, examining the intricate symbolism, and considering the theological significance, we open ourselves to a fuller understanding of this remarkable biblical text.

The Book of Daniel challenges us to see beyond the surface, to seek the deeper truths that lie beneath the symbolic language. It calls us to trust in God's sovereignty, to remain faithful in the face of trials, and to hold fast to the hope of His ultimate victory. As we unpack the prophetic symbols in Daniel, may we be inspired to live with greater faith, understanding, and anticipation of God's unfolding plan.

In the chapters that follow, we will journey through the visions and symbols of Daniel, uncovering their meanings and implications. Let us begin this exploration with open hearts and minds, ready to be transformed by the timeless truths contained within this extraordinary book.

xi

DR. MAXWELL SHIMBA

CHAPTER 01

THE HISTORICAL CONTEXT OF DANIEL

Understanding the historical backdrop of the Book of Daniel is crucial for grasping its prophetic symbols. This chapter explores the Babylonian exile, the rise of the Medo-Persian Empire, and the cultural and political milieu in which Daniel lived and prophesied. It also examines the significance of Daniel's role in the royal courts of Babylon and Persia.

The Babylonian Exile

The Babylonian exile is a pivotal event in Jewish history, marking a period of profound transformation and upheaval. In 586 B.C., the Babylonian king Nebuchadnezzar II conquered Jerusalem, destroyed the Temple, and deported a significant portion of the Jewish population to Babylon. This event not only disrupted the social and religious life of the Jewish people but also challenged their identity and faith.

For the exiles, living in a foreign land under a powerful empire presented numerous challenges. They had to navigate the complexities of maintaining their religious practices and cultural identity while being subjected to the dominant Babylonian culture. This period of exile is the backdrop against which the Book of Daniel is set, and it profoundly influences the themes and messages of the book.

Daniel and His Companions

Daniel, along with his companions Hananiah, Mishael, and Azariah (known by their Babylonian names Shadrach, Meshach, and Abednego), were among the young Jewish nobles taken into Babylonian captivity. Selected for their intelligence and potential, they were enrolled in a rigorous training program designed to prepare them for service in the royal court. This education included learning the language and literature of the Babylonians, a process aimed at assimilating them into Babylonian society.

Despite the pressures to conform, Daniel and his friends remained steadfast in their commitment to their faith. Their refusal to eat the king's food, opting instead for a diet that adhered to their religious laws, is an early indication of their resolve. This act of faith not only preserved their identity but also earned them favor and respect in the eyes of their captors.

The Rise of the Medo-Persian Empire

The fall of Babylon in 539 B.C. to the Medo-Persian Empire, led by Cyrus the Great, marked another significant shift in the historical context of Daniel. The Medo-Persian Empire was characterized by a more lenient approach to its conquered peoples, allowing for greater religious and cultural autonomy. Cyrus's decree, permitting the Jewish exiles to return to their homeland and rebuild the Temple, is a testament to this policy.

Daniel's role in the court transitioned seamlessly from the Babylonian to the Persian administration. His continued service under Darius the Mede and later Cyrus the Persian indicates his esteemed position and the high regard in which he was held. This continuity of service across different regimes underscores the divine favor and protection over Daniel's life and mission.

The Cultural and Political Milieu

The cultural and political milieu of the time was marked by significant developments in governance, religion, and philosophy. The Babylonian Empire was known for its advancements in astronomy, mathematics, and literature. The royal court was a center of intellectual activity, attracting scholars and wise men from various regions.

Religiously, the Babylonians practiced polytheism, worshiping a pantheon of gods with Marduk as the chief deity.

The presence of multiple religious beliefs and practices created a complex environment for the Jewish exiles, who were monotheistic and strictly adhered to the worship of Yahweh.

Politically, the transition from Babylonian to Persian rule brought about changes in administration and policy. The Persian Empire, with its vast expanse and diverse population, implemented a system of satrapies or provinces, each governed by a satrap. This decentralized form of governance allowed for more localized control and fostered a degree of stability and order across the empire.

Daniel's Role in the Royal Courts

Daniel's role in the royal courts of both Babylon and Persia is a testament to his wisdom, integrity, and unwavering faith. In the Babylonian court, Daniel rose to prominence by interpreting King Nebuchadnezzar's dreams, which none of the other wise men could decipher. His accurate interpretation and subsequent promotion to a high-ranking position demonstrated his exceptional abilities and divine insight.

Under Persian rule, Daniel continued to serve with distinction. His appointment as one of the three administrators overseeing the satraps under King Darius the Mede highlights his trusted position. Daniel's integrity and dedication to his duties earned him the envy of other officials, leading to the infamous plot against him that resulted in his being thrown into the lion's den. Miraculously spared by divine intervention, Daniel's faith and God's deliverance further solidified his reputation and influence.

The Significance of Daniel's Prophecies

Daniel's prophecies are deeply intertwined with the historical and political contexts of his time. His visions often reflected the rise and fall of empires, symbolized by various beasts and images. These prophecies provided not only a divine perspective on contemporary events but also a glimpse into the future, offering hope and assurance of God's sovereign plan.

For the Jewish exiles, Daniel's prophecies served as a reminder of God's control over history and His promise of eventual restoration. The symbolic language and vivid imagery used in the visions reinforced the message that despite current adversities, God's kingdom would ultimately prevail.

Conclusion

The historical context of the Book of Daniel is essential for understanding its prophetic symbols. The Babylonian exile, the rise of the Medo-Persian Empire, and the cultural and political environment in which Daniel lived and prophesied provide a rich backdrop for his visions. Daniel's remarkable journey from a captive in Babylon to a prominent figure in the Persian court underscores the themes of faithfulness, divine favor, and the sovereignty of God.

As we delve deeper into the prophetic symbols in the subsequent chapters, this historical foundation will help us appreciate the profound messages and timeless truths embedded in the Book of Daniel.

PROPHETIC SYMBOLS AND IMAGES IN DANIEL CHAPTER 2

Daniel Chapter 2 presents one of the most detailed and compelling visions in the Book of Daniel. In this chapter, King Nebuchadnezzar of Babylon has a troubling dream that none of his wise men can interpret. Daniel, through divine revelation, can both recount and interpret the dream, revealing a prophetic timeline of world empires leading to the establishment of God's eternal kingdom. This chapter delves into the prophetic symbols and images in Nebuchadnezzar's dream, offering comprehensive commentary and biblical references to uncover their profound meanings.

Nebuchadnezzar's Dream: The Statue

The Statue and Its Parts

1. The Head of Gold

Symbol: Babylonian Empire

Meaning: The head of gold represents King Nebuchadnezzar and the Babylonian Empire. Gold, a precious and highly valued metal, symbolizes the wealth, power, and splendor of Babylon during Nebuchadnezzar's reign.

References: Daniel 2:37-38 - "You, O king, are a king of kings. For the God of heaven has given you a kingdom, power, strength, and glory; and wherever the children of men dwell, or the beasts of the field and the birds of the heaven, He has given them into your hand, and has made you ruler over them all—you are this head of gold."

Strong's Concordance: The term "gold" (H1722 - zahab) often symbolizes great value and purity, indicating the unrivaled supremacy of Babylon at the time.

2. The Chest and Arms of Silver

Symbol: Medo-Persian Empire

Meaning: The chest and arms of silver represent the Medo-Persian Empire, which succeeded Babylon. Silver, though valuable, is inferior to gold, symbolizing a kingdom of great power but less glory than Babylon.

References: Daniel 2:39 - "But after you shall arise another kingdom inferior to yours; then another, a third kingdom of bronze, which shall rule over all the earth."

Strong's Concordance: The term "silver" (H3701 - keseph) signifies value but lesser purity and strength compared to gold, highlighting the Medo-Persian Empire's prominent yet secondary status.

3. The Belly and Thighs of Bronze

Symbol: Greek Empire

Meaning: The belly and thighs of bronze symbolize the Greek Empire under Alexander the Great. Bronze, known for its strength and durability, represents the widespread influence and military prowess of Greece.

References: Daniel 2:39 - "...then another, a third kingdom of bronze, which shall rule over all the earth."

Strong's Concordance: The term "bronze" (H5174 - nechash) often symbolizes firmness and endurance, reflecting the extensive and robust nature of the Greek Empire.

4. The Legs of Iron

Symbol: Roman Empire

Meaning: The legs of iron represent the Roman Empire. Iron, a strong and unyielding metal, symbolizes the might and extensive control of Rome, which crushed and subdued all other kingdoms.

References: Daniel 2:40 - "And the fourth kingdom shall be as strong as iron, inasmuch as iron breaks in pieces and shatters everything; and like iron that crushes, that kingdom will break in pieces and crush all the others."

Strong's Concordance: The term "iron" (H6523 - parzel) indicates strength and destructive power, reflecting Rome's dominance and harsh rule.

5. The Feet Partly of Iron and Partly of Clay

Symbol: Divided Kingdoms

Meaning: The feet partly of iron and partly of clay symbolize the divided nature of the kingdoms that followed the Roman Empire. The mixture of iron and clay indicates a kingdom with elements of strength (iron) and weakness (clay), unable to fully unite.

References: Daniel 2:41-43 - "Whereas you saw the feet and toes, partly of potter's clay and partly of iron, the kingdom shall be divided; yet the strength of the iron shall be in it, just as you saw the iron mixed with ceramic clay. And as the toes of the feet were partly of iron and partly of clay, so the kingdom shall be partly strong and partly fragile."

Strong's Concordance: The term "clay" (H2635 - chasaph) signifies fragility and instability, highlighting the inherent weaknesses and disunity of the post-Roman kingdoms.

The Stone Cut Without Hands

The Stone and Its Impact

Symbol: The Kingdom of God

Meaning: The stone cut without hands represents the divine kingdom established by God, which will destroy all earthly kingdoms and endure forever. The fact that it is cut without hands signifies its divine origin, not made by human effort.

References: Daniel 2:34-35 - "You watched while a stone was cut out without hands, which struck the image on its feet of iron and clay, and broke them in pieces. Then the iron, the clay, the bronze, the silver, and the gold were crushed together, and became like chaff from the summer threshing floors; the wind carried them away so that no trace of them was found. And the stone that struck the image became a great mountain and filled the whole earth."

Strong's Concordance: The term "stone" (H68 - eben) often signifies a cornerstone or foundational element, pointing to Christ as the cornerstone of God's eternal kingdom (see Psalm 118:22; Ephesians 2:20).

Interpretation and Prophetic Meaning

Divine Revelation to Daniel

Daniel 2:19 - "Then the secret was revealed to Daniel in a night vision. So Daniel blessed the God of heaven."

Daniel's ability to interpret the dream was a result of divine revelation, highlighting the prophetic nature of his interpretation. This divine insight not only underscored Daniel's prophetic gift but also validated the truth and authority of the vision.

The Eternal Kingdom

Daniel 2:44-45 - "And in the days of these kings the God of heaven will set up a kingdom which shall never be destroyed; and the kingdom shall not be left to other people; it shall break in pieces and consume all these kingdoms, and it shall stand forever. Inasmuch as you saw that the stone was cut out of the mountain without hands, and that it broke in pieces the iron, the bronze, the clay, the silver, and the gold— the great God has made known to the king what will come to pass after this. The dream is certain, and its interpretation is sure."

The culmination of the vision is the establishment of God's eternal kingdom, which will supplant all human kingdoms. This kingdom, symbolized by the stone, is everlasting and unshakeable, representing the ultimate fulfillment of God's redemptive plan.

Conclusion

Daniel Chapter 2 provides a sweeping prophetic overview of the major empires of human history, culminating in the establishment of God's eternal kingdom. The statue, with its various metals, symbolizes the succession of world empires from Babylon to the divided kingdoms that followed Rome. The stone cut without hands represents the divine kingdom that will ultimately prevail. Through careful analysis of these symbols and their meanings, we gain a deeper understanding of God's sovereign control over history and the assured victory of His eternal kingdom.

As we move forward in our study, this foundational vision will serve as a key reference point for interpreting the subsequent prophetic symbols in the Book of Daniel. The historical and theological insights gleaned from this chapter provide a robust framework for understanding the unfolding of God's divine plan.

CHAPTER 03

PROPHETIC SYMBOLS AND IMAGES IN DANIEL CHAPTER 4

Daniel Chapter 4 is a unique and intriguing chapter in the Book of Daniel, presenting a detailed account of King Nebuchadnezzar's second dream and its interpretation by Daniel. This chapter explores the prophetic literature, symbols, and images within the dream, offering an expository study and comprehensive commentary supported by Bible verses and insights from Strong's Concordance.

Nebuchadnezzar's Dream: The Great Tree

The Dream Described

Daniel 4:10-12 - "These were the visions of my head while on my bed: I was looking, and behold, a tree in the midst of the earth, and its height was great. The tree grew and became strong; its height reached to the heavens, and it could be seen to the ends of all the earth. Its leaves were lovely, its fruit abundant, and in it was food for all. The beasts of the field found shade under it, the birds of the heavens dwelt in its branches, and all flesh was fed from it."

The Symbols in Nebuchadnezzar's Dream

1. The Great Tree

Symbol: Nebuchadnezzar and His Kingdom

Meaning: The great tree represents King Nebuchadnezzar and his vast kingdom. The tree's height and its visibility from all ends of the earth signify the extensive reach and influence of Nebuchadnezzar's rule. The abundant fruit and shade provided by the tree symbolize the prosperity and protection his kingdom offered to its inhabitants.

Strong's Concordance: The term "tree" (H363 - `ilan) is often used to symbolize strength and growth. In prophetic literature, trees can represent nations or leaders (see Ezekiel 31:3, 5-6; Isaiah 2:13).

References: Daniel 4:20-22 - "The tree that you saw, which grew and became strong, whose height reached to the heavens and which could be seen by all the earth, whose leaves were lovely and its fruit abundant, in which was food for all, under which the beasts of the field dwelt, and in whose branches the birds of the heaven had their home—it is you, O king, who have grown and become strong; for your greatness has grown and reaches to the heavens, and your dominion to the end of the earth."

2. The Watcher and the Holy One

Symbol: Divine Messengers

Meaning: The watcher and the holy one descending from heaven represent divine messengers or angels. Their decree to chop down the tree symbolizes God's judgment upon Nebuchadnezzar for his pride and arrogance.

Strong's Concordance: The term "watcher" (H5894 - `iyr) is derived from a root meaning "to be wakeful." It denotes a vigilant guardian, often referring to angels in biblical literature.

References: Daniel 4:13-14 - "I saw in the visions of my head while on my bed, and there was a watcher, a holy one, coming down from heaven. He cried aloud and said thus: 'Chop down the tree and cut off its branches, strip off its leaves and scatter its fruit. Let the beasts get out from under it, and the birds from its branches.'"

3. The Stump with Bands of Iron and Bronze

Symbol: Preservation and Future Restoration

Meaning: The stump with bands of iron and bronze signifies that although Nebuchadnezzar's kingdom would be stripped from him, his life would be preserved, and there would be a future restoration. The bands of iron and bronze represent the confinement and restraint placed upon Nebuchadnezzar during his period of madness.

Strong's Concordance: The term "stump" (H6136 - `iqr) symbolizes something remaining after destruction, indicating hope for future regrowth.

References: Daniel 4:15 - "Nevertheless leave the stump and roots in the earth, bound with a band of iron and bronze, in the tender grass of the field. Let it be wet with the dew of heaven, and let him graze with the beasts on the grass of the earth."

4. The Seven Times

Symbol: Period of Judgment

Meaning: The "seven times" refers to a period of seven years during which Nebuchadnezzar would live as a beast, stripped of his royal dignity and sanity. This time of judgment was intended to humble Nebuchadnezzar and lead him to acknowledge God's sovereignty.

Strong's Concordance: The term "times" (H5732 - `iddan) denotes a fixed period or season, often used to signify a specific duration in prophetic contexts.

References: Daniel 4:16 - "Let his heart be changed from that of a man, let him be given the heart of a beast, and let seven times pass over him."

Daniel's Interpretation and Prophetic Meaning

Divine Revelation to Daniel

Daniel 4:19 - "Then Daniel, whose name was Belteshazzar, was astonished for a time, and his thoughts troubled him. So the king spoke, and said, 'Belteshazzar, do not let the dream or its interpretation trouble you.' Belteshazzar answered and said, 'My lord, may the dream concern those who hate you, and its interpretation concern your enemies!'"

Daniel's reaction to the dream indicates the seriousness of the message. His initial reluctance to convey the interpretation underscores the severity of the judgment pronounced upon Nebuchadnezzar.

The Judgment Pronounced

Daniel 4:24-26 - "This is the interpretation, O king, and this is the decree of the Most High, which has come upon my lord the king: They shall drive you from men, your dwelling shall be with the beasts of the field, and they shall make you eat grass like oxen. They shall wet you with the dew of heaven, and seven times shall pass over you, till you know that the Most High rules in the kingdom of men, and gives it to whomever He chooses. And inasmuch as they gave the command to leave the stump and roots of the tree, your kingdom shall be assured to you, after you come to know that Heaven rules."

Daniel interprets the dream as a divine decree of judgment upon Nebuchadnezzar for his pride. The king's fall from power and descent into madness serve as a humbling experience, designed to teach him that God is sovereign over all kingdoms.

The Fulfillment of the Dream

Daniel 4:28-33 - "All this came upon King Nebuchadnezzar. At the end of the twelve months he was walking about the royal palace of Babylon. The king spoke, saying, 'Is not this great Babylon, that I have built for a royal dwelling by my mighty power and for the honor of my majesty?' While the word was still in the king's mouth, a voice fell from heaven: 'King Nebuchadnezzar, to you it is spoken: the kingdom has departed from you! And they shall drive you from men, and your dwelling shall be with the beasts of the field. They shall make you eat grass like oxen; and seven times shall pass over you, until you know that the Most High rules in the kingdom of men, and gives it to whomever He chooses.' That very hour the word was fulfilled concerning Nebuchadnezzar; he was driven from men and ate grass like oxen; his body was wet with the dew of heaven till his hair had grown like eagles' feathers and his nails like birds' claws."

The prophecy is fulfilled exactly as Daniel interpreted. Nebuchadnezzar's prideful declaration about his achievements triggers the immediate execution of the divine judgment. He is driven from human society and lives as a beast for seven years, experiencing the humbling that leads him to recognize God's sovereignty.

Nebuchadnezzar's Restoration and Praise

Daniel 4:34-37 - "And at the end of the time, I, Nebuchadnezzar, lifted my eyes to heaven, and my understanding returned to me; and I blessed the Most High and praised and honored Him who lives forever: For His dominion is an everlasting dominion, and His kingdom is from generation to generation. All the inhabitants of the earth are reputed as nothing; He does according to His will in the army of heaven and among the inhabitants of the earth. No one can restrain His hand or say to Him, 'What have You done?' At the same time my reason returned to me, and for the glory of my kingdom, my honor and splendor returned to me. My counselors and nobles resorted to me, I was restored to my kingdom, and excellent majesty was added to me. Now I, Nebuchadnezzar, praise and extol and honor the King of heaven, all of whose works are truth, and His ways justice. And those who walk in pride He is able to put down."

After the period of judgment, Nebuchadnezzar's sanity and royal dignity are restored. He responds with a profound declaration of praise and recognition of God's eternal dominion. This acknowledgment of divine sovereignty marks a significant transformation in Nebuchadnezzar's character and reign.

Theological and Prophetic Implications

The Sovereignty of God

The central theme of Daniel Chapter 4 is the sovereignty of God over human affairs. The judgment upon Nebuchadnezzar serves as a powerful reminder that all earthly power and authority are subordinate to the will of the Most High. God's ability to humble the proud and exalt the humble is vividly illustrated through Nebuchadnezzar's experience.

References: Proverbs 16:18 - "Pride goes before destruction, and a haughty spirit before a fall."

The Purpose of Divine Judgment

The purpose of divine judgment, as seen in Nebuchadnezzar's dream and its fulfillment, is to bring about repentance and recognition of God's authority. Nebuchadnezzar's humbling serves as a corrective measure, leading him to a greater understanding and acknowledgment of God's supreme rule.

References: Hebrews 12:6 - "For whom the Lord loves He chastens, and scourges every son whom He receives."

Conclusion

Daniel Chapter 4 provides a rich tapestry of prophetic symbols and images, each conveying profound theological truths. The great tree, the watcher and holy one, the stump with bands of iron and bronze, and the seven times all serve to illustrate the themes of divine judgment, humility, and the sovereignty of God. Through a detailed examination of these symbols and their interpretation by Daniel, we gain a deeper understanding of God's dealings with humanity and His ultimate authority over all creation.

As we continue our exploration of the prophetic symbols in the Book of Daniel, this chapter's insights into God's sovereignty and the purpose of divine judgment will serve as foundational principles, guiding our interpretation of the subsequent visions and prophecies.

CHAPTER 04

PROPHETIC SYMBOLS AND IMAGES IN DANIEL CHAPTER 5

Daniel Chapter 5 recounts the dramatic and prophetic events of King Belshazzar's feast, culminating in the mysterious writing on the wall and its interpretation by Daniel. This chapter explores the prophetic symbols, images, and messages within the narrative, offering detailed interpretations and their meanings. Special attention is given to the prophetic significance of the words written on the wall, the colors mentioned, and the symbolic meaning of Daniel's clothing and adornments.

The Feast of Belshazzar

The Profane Use of Sacred Vessels

Daniel 5:1-4 - "Belshazzar the king made a great feast for a thousand of his lords, and drank wine in the presence of the thousand. While he tasted the wine, Belshazzar gave the command to bring the gold and silver vessels which his father Nebuchadnezzar had taken from the temple which had been in Jerusalem, that the king and his lords, his wives, and his concubines might drink from them. Then they brought the gold vessels that had been taken from the temple of the house of God which had been in Jerusalem; and the king and his lords, his wives, and his concubines drank from them. They drank wine, and praised the gods of gold and silver, bronze and iron, wood and stone."

Symbol: The profane use of sacred vessels.

Meaning: The act of using the sacred vessels from the Jerusalem temple for a pagan feast symbolizes the utter disrespect and sacrilege of Belshazzar towards the God of Israel. This act of desecration highlights the king's arrogance and irreverence, setting the stage for divine judgment.

References: Exodus 30:29 - "You shall consecrate them, that they may be most holy; whatever touches them must be holy."

Strong's Concordance: The term "vessel" (H3627 - keliy) signifies an instrument or a tool, often used in religious contexts to denote items dedicated to sacred use.

The Writing on the Wall

The Mysterious Hand and the Inscription

Daniel 5:5-6 - "In the same hour the fingers of a man's hand appeared and wrote opposite the lampstand on the plaster of the wall of the king's palace, and the king saw the part of the hand that wrote. Then the king's countenance changed, and his thoughts troubled him, so that the joints of his hips were loosened and his knees knocked against each other."

Symbol: The fingers of a man's hand.

Meaning: The appearance of the mysterious handwriting on the wall is a direct divine intervention, symbolizing God's immediate judgment and the revelation of His will. The supernatural nature of the event underscores the seriousness of the message.

Strong's Concordance: The term "hand" (H3027 - yad) often symbolizes power and authority. The divine hand signifies God's direct intervention in human affairs.

The Words Written on the Wall

Daniel 5:25-28 - "And this is the inscription that was written: MENE, MENE, TEKEL, UPHARSIN. This is the interpretation of each word. MENE: God has numbered your kingdom, and finished it; TEKEL: You have been weighed in the balances, and found wanting; PERES: Your kingdom has been divided, and given to the Medes and Persians."

1. MENE

Symbol: Numbered.

Meaning: The repetition of the word "MENE" emphasizes the certainty and finality of God's decree. God has numbered the days of Belshazzar's kingdom and determined that it has come to an end.

Strong's Concordance: The term "MENE" (H4484 - menah) means to number or reckon.

2. TEKEL

Symbol: Weighed.

Meaning: "TEKEL" indicates that Belshazzar has been weighed in the divine scales and found deficient. His actions and character have been judged and found lacking in righteousness and integrity.

Strong's Concordance: The term "TEKEL" (H8625 - teqal) means to weigh.

3. PERES / UPHARSIN

Symbol: Divided.

Meaning: The word "PERES" (singular of "UPHARSIN") signifies the division and subsequent destruction of Belshazzar's kingdom. It foretells the transfer of power to the Medes and Persians.

Strong's Concordance: The term "PERES" (H6537 - peras) means to divide or split. "UPHARSIN" (H6536 -

parac) refers to the plural form, indicating a division among multiple entities.

The Colors and Symbols of the Feast

The Mention of Colors

Daniel 5:7 - "The king cried aloud to bring in the astrologers, the Chaldeans, and the soothsayers. The king spoke, saying to the wise men of Babylon, 'Whoever reads this writing, and tells me its interpretation, shall be clothed with purple and have a chain of gold around his neck; and he shall be the third ruler in the kingdom.'"

Symbol: The use of colors, particularly purple and gold.

Meaning: The color purple, traditionally associated with royalty and nobility, symbolizes wealth, power, and high status. The gold chain signifies honor, authority, and distinction. These rewards promised by Belshazzar indicate the high value placed on deciphering the mysterious inscription.

Strong's Concordance: The term "purple" (H713 - argaman) denotes a color associated with royalty. The term "gold" (H2091 - zahab) signifies wealth and purity.

Daniel's Interpretation and Reward

Daniel's Prophetic Interpretation

Daniel 5:17-28 - "Then Daniel answered, and said before the king, 'Let your gifts be for yourself and give your rewards to another; yet I will read the writing to the king, and make known to him the interpretation. O king, the Most High God gave Nebuchadnezzar your father a kingdom and majesty, glory and honor. And because of the majesty that He gave him, all peoples, nations, and languages trembled and feared before him. Whomever he wished, he executed; whomever he wished, he kept alive; whomever he wished, he set up; and whomever he wished, he put down. But when his heart was lifted up, and his spirit was hardened in pride, he was deposed from his kingly throne, and they took his glory from him. Then he was driven from the sons of men, his heart was made like the beasts, and his dwelling was with the wild donkeys. They fed him with grass like oxen, and his body was wet with the dew of heaven, till he knew that the Most High God rules in the kingdom of men, and appoints over it whomever He chooses. But you his son, Belshazzar, have not humbled your heart, although you knew all this. And you have lifted yourself up against the Lord of heaven. They have brought the vessels of His house before you, and you and your lords, your wives and your concubines, have drunk wine from them. And you have praised the gods of silver and gold, bronze and iron, wood and stone, which do not see or hear or know; and the God who holds your breath in His hand and owns all your ways, you have not glorified. Then the fingers of the hand were sent from Him, and this writing was written. And this is the inscription that was written: MENE, MENE, TEKEL, UPHARSIN.'"

Daniel's interpretation underscores Belshazzar's pride and failure to learn from Nebuchadnezzar's humbling experience. The prophetic meaning of the writing on the wall is a direct judgment of Belshazzar's arrogance and sacrilege.

Daniel's Reward and Its Prophetic Significance

Daniel 5:29 - "Then Belshazzar gave the command, and they clothed Daniel with purple and put a chain of gold around his neck, and made a proclamation concerning him that he should be the third ruler in the kingdom."

Symbol: Purple clothing and a gold chain.

Meaning: The purple clothing and gold chain symbolize honor, authority, and high status bestowed upon Daniel. However, these rewards also carry prophetic significance. Despite being honored by an earthly king, Daniel's ultimate loyalty and service are to the Most High God. The temporary nature of Belshazzar's kingdom contrasts with the eternal kingdom of God, which Daniel faithfully represents.

Strong's Concordance: The term "purple" (H713 - argaman) and "gold" (H2091 - zahab) highlight the regal and honorable status conferred upon Daniel.

Prophetic Meaning: Daniel's adornment with purple and gold signifies his recognition and honor by earthly powers, yet it foreshadows the transient nature of human kingdoms in contrast to the enduring kingdom of God. Daniel's elevation in the Babylonian court prefigures the ultimate vindication and exaltation of God's faithful servants in His eternal kingdom.

The Fall of Babylon

Daniel 5:30-31 - "That very night Belshazzar, king of the Chaldeans, was slain. And Darius the Mede received the kingdom, being about sixty-two years old."

The swift fulfillment of the prophecy underscores the certainty and immediacy of God's judgment. The fall of Babylon to Darius the Mede marks the transition from the Babylonian Empire to the Medo-Persian Empire, as foretold in the prophetic writings.

References: Isaiah

47:11 - "Therefore evil shall come upon you; you shall not know from where it arises. And trouble shall fall upon you; you will not be able to put it off. And desolation shall come upon you suddenly, which you shall not know."

Conclusion

Daniel Chapter 5 presents a vivid narrative rich with prophetic symbols and images. The mysterious writing on the wall, the colors of the garments, and the gold chain all carry deep prophetic meanings. Through Daniel's interpretation and the subsequent fulfillment of the prophecy, we see the themes of divine judgment, the transient nature of human power, and the ultimate sovereignty of God.

The prophetic symbols and messages in this chapter serve as a powerful reminder of God's control over the affairs of nations and individuals. As we continue our study of the Book of Daniel, the insights from this chapter will deepen our understanding of the broader prophetic landscape and God's unfolding plan for history.

CHAPTER 05

PROPHETIC SYMBOLS AND IMAGES IN DANIEL CHAPTER 6

Daniel Chapter 6 is one of the most famous chapters in the Book of Daniel, detailing the story of Daniel in the lion's den. This chapter explores the prophetic literature, symbols, and images within this narrative, with a particular focus on the lions. By examining the meanings and prophetic significance of the lions and other symbols in this chapter, we gain a deeper understanding of the divine messages conveyed through Daniel's experiences.

The Plot Against Daniel

The Jealous Officials

Daniel 6:1-5 - "It pleased Darius to set over the kingdom one hundred and twenty satraps, to be over the whole kingdom; and over these, three governors, of whom Daniel was one, that the satraps might give account to them so that the king would suffer no loss. Then Daniel distinguished himself above the governors and satraps because an excellent spirit was in him, and the king gave thought to setting him over the whole realm. So the governors and satraps sought to find some charge against Daniel concerning the kingdom; but they could find no charge or fault, because he was faithful; nor was there any error or fault found in him. Then these men said, 'We shall not find any charge against this Daniel unless we find it against him concerning the law of his God.'"

Symbol: The conspiracy against Daniel.

Meaning: The plot by the officials symbolizes the inevitable conflict between righteousness and worldly powers. Daniel's integrity and faithfulness to God make him a target for those who are envious and corrupt. This conflict sets the stage for a demonstration of God's power and protection.

References: Psalm 37:32 - "The wicked watches the righteous, and seeks to slay him."

The Decree and Daniel's Faithfulness

The Decree of King Darius

Daniel 6:6-9 - "So these governors and satraps thronged before the king, and said thus to him: 'King Darius, live forever! All the governors of the kingdom, the administrators and satraps, the counselors and advisors, have consulted together to establish a royal statute and to make a firm decree, that whoever petitions any god or man for thirty days, except you, O king, shall be cast into the den of lions. Now, O king, establish the decree and sign the writing, so that it cannot be changed, according to the law of the Medes and Persians, which does not alter.' Therefore King Darius signed the written decree."

Symbol: The unchangeable decree.

Meaning: The decree represents the rigidity and fallibility of human laws compared to the supreme and unchanging laws of God. The manipulation of King Darius by the officials underscores the vulnerability of human authority to deception and malice.

References: Esther 1:19 - "If it pleases the king, let a royal decree go out from him, and let it be recorded in the laws of the Persians and the Medes, so that it will not be altered..."

Daniel's Faithfulness

Daniel 6:10 - "Now when Daniel knew that the writing was signed, he went home. And in his upper room, with his windows open toward Jerusalem, he knelt down on his knees three times that day, and prayed and gave thanks before his God, as was his custom since early days."

Symbol: Daniel's prayer.

Meaning: Daniel's unwavering commitment to prayer symbolizes steadfast faith and devotion to God, even in the face of severe persecution. His actions demonstrate the importance of maintaining spiritual disciplines regardless of external pressures.

References: 1 Kings 8:48 - "And when they return to You with all their heart and with all their soul in the land of their enemies who led them away captive and pray to You toward their land which You gave to their fathers, the city which You have chosen and the temple which I have built for Your name."

Daniel in the Lion's Den

The Lions' Den

Daniel 6:16-17 - "So the king gave the command, and they brought Daniel and cast him into the den of lions. But the king spoke, saying to Daniel, 'Your God, whom you serve continually, He will deliver you.' Then a stone was brought and laid on the mouth of the den, and the king sealed it with his own signet ring and with the signets of his lords, that the purpose concerning Daniel might not be changed."

Symbol: The lions' den.

Meaning: The lions' den symbolizes a place of ultimate trial and testing. It represents the extreme dangers and life-threatening situations that believers may face because of their faith. The sealing of the den with the king's signet highlights the perceived finality and inescapability of Daniel's predicament.

Strong's Concordance: The term "lion" (H744 - 'ariy) often symbolizes strength, power, and danger. In prophetic literature, lions can represent oppressive forces or adversaries.

References: Psalm 22:21 - "Save Me from the lion's mouth and from the horns of the wild oxen! You have answered Me."

The Deliverance of Daniel

Daniel 6:19-22 - "Then the king arose very early in the morning and went in haste to the den of lions. And when he came to the den, he cried out with a lamenting voice to Daniel. The king spoke, saying to Daniel, 'Daniel, servant of the living God, has your God, whom you serve continually, been able to deliver you from the lions?' Then Daniel said to the king, 'O king, live forever! My God sent His angel and shut the lions' mouths, so that they have not hurt me, because I was found innocent before Him; and also, O king, I have done no wrong before you.'"

Symbol: The shut mouths of the lions.

Meaning: The shutting of the lions' mouths by an angel symbolizes divine protection and the power of God to save His faithful servants from seemingly impossible situations. It also signifies the vindication of Daniel's innocence and God's supremacy over natural forces and human schemes.

Strong's Concordance: The term "angel" (H4397 - mal'ak) refers to a messenger or divine being sent by God to carry out His purposes.

References: Psalm 91:11 - "For He shall give His angels charge over you, to keep you in all your ways."

The Fate of the Accusers

Daniel 6:24 - "And the king gave the command, and they brought those men who had accused Daniel, and they cast them into the den of lions—them, their children, and their wives; and the lions overpowered them, and broke all their bones in pieces before they ever came to the bottom of the den."

Symbol: The judgment upon the accusers.

Meaning: The fate of the accusers symbolizes the principle of divine justice and retribution. Those who sought to harm Daniel were themselves destroyed by the very danger they intended for him. This reversal of fortune highlights the righteousness of God's judgment and the ultimate triumph of the faithful over their enemies.

References: Proverbs 26:27 - "Whoever digs a pit will fall into it, and he who rolls a stone will have it roll back on him."

Daniel's Recognition and Prophetic Significance

Daniel's Elevation and the King's Decree

Daniel 6:25-28 - "Then King Darius wrote: 'To all peoples, nations, and languages that dwell in all the earth: Peace be multiplied to you. I make a decree that in every dominion of my kingdom men must tremble and fear before the God of Daniel. For He is the living God, and steadfast forever; His kingdom is the one which shall not be destroyed, and His dominion shall endure to the end. He delivers and rescues, and He works signs and wonders in heaven and on earth, who has delivered Daniel from the power of the lions.' So this Daniel prospered in the reign of Darius and in the reign of Cyrus the Persian."

Symbol: The king's decree and Daniel's prosperity.

Meaning: The decree by King Darius symbolizes the recognition of God's sovereignty and the acknowledgment of His power and deliverance. Daniel's continued prosperity under Darius and Cyrus signifies the ongoing favor and blessing of God upon His faithful servant. It also points to the ultimate triumph and vindication of those who remain steadfast in their faith.

References: Daniel 2:44 - "And in the days of these kings the God of heaven will set up a kingdom which shall never be destroyed; and the kingdom shall not be left to other people; it shall break in pieces and consume all these kingdoms, and it shall stand forever."

The Prophetic Meaning of Lions

Symbolism of Lions in Biblical Literature

Lions often symbolize power, strength, and danger in biblical literature. They can represent both the righteous and the wicked, depending on the context. For instance, lions symbolize the tribe of Judah and the Messiah in positive contexts, while they represent adversaries and destructive forces in negative contexts.

References:

- Genesis 49:9 - "Judah is a lion's whelp; from the prey, my son, you have gone up. He bows down, he lies down as a lion; and as a lion, who shall rouse him?"

- 1 Peter 5:8 - "Be sober, be vigilant; because your adversary the devil walks about like a roaring lion, seeking whom he may devour."

Prophetic Meaning in Daniel 6

In Daniel 6, the lions symbolize the life-threatening trials and adversaries that believers may face. However, their inability to harm Daniel represents God's power to protect and deliver His faithful servants. This deliverance serves as a prophetic message of hope and assurance that God is in control, even in the most perilous situations.

Conclusion

Daniel Chapter 6 provides a rich narrative filled with prophetic symbols and images. The lions' den, the decree of King Darius, and the miraculous deliverance of Daniel all convey profound theological and prophetic messages. Through Daniel's faithfulness and God's intervention, we see the themes of divine protection, the triumph of faith, and the ultimate justice of God.

The lions in this chapter symbolize both the dangers faced by believers and the power of God to protect and deliver. The narrative serves as a powerful reminder of God's sovereignty and the assurance that He watches over His faithful servants. As we continue to explore the prophetic symbols in the Book of Daniel, the insights from this chapter will deepen our understanding of God's purposes and His unwavering commitment to His people.

CHAPTER 06

THE FOUR BEASTS AND THE KINGDOMS OF THE WORLD (DANIEL 7)

Daniel Chapter 7 presents a vivid and symbolic vision that has intrigued scholars and believers for centuries. In this chapter, the prophet Daniel envisions four beasts rising from the sea, each representing a significant kingdom in world history. This chapter will focus on the first beast, the lion with eagle's wings, symbolizing the Babylonian Empire. We will explore the prophetic literature, symbols, and images associated with this vision, offering a comprehensive commentary and interpretation supported by Bible verses and insights from Strong's Concordance.

Daniel's Vision of the Four Beasts

Daniel 7:1-3 - "In the first year of Belshazzar king of Babylon, Daniel had a dream and visions of his head while on his bed. Then he wrote down the dream, telling the main facts.

Daniel spoke, saying, 'I saw in my vision by night, and behold, the four winds of heaven were stirring up the Great Sea. And four great beasts came up from the sea, each different from the other.'"

The vision takes place in the first year of Belshazzar's reign, setting the historical context for the vision. The four winds of heaven stirring up the Great Sea symbolize the chaotic and tumultuous events that give rise to these powerful kingdoms.

The First Beast: The Lion with Eagle's Wings

Daniel 7:4 - "The first was like a lion, and had eagle's wings. I watched till its wings were plucked off; and it was lifted up from the earth and made to stand on two feet like a man, and a man's heart was given to it."

The Symbolism of the Lion with Eagle's Wings

1. The Lion

Symbol: Babylonian Empire.

Meaning: The lion, known as the king of beasts, symbolizes the power, strength, and dominance of the Babylonian Empire. Lions were commonly associated with royalty and power in the ancient Near East, and this imagery is fitting for the mighty Babylonian kingdom under Nebuchadnezzar.

Strong's Concordance: The term "lion" (H744 - 'ariy) is often used in the Bible to symbolize strength and royalty (e.g., Genesis 49:9, Ezekiel 19:2).

References: Jeremiah 4:7 - "The lion has come up from his thicket, and the destroyer of nations is on his way. He has gone forth from his place to make your land desolate; your cities will be laid waste, without inhabitant."

2. The Eagle's Wings

Symbol: Speed and Conquest.

Meaning: The eagle's wings represent the swift and far-reaching conquests of the Babylonian Empire. Eagles, known for their keen sight and swift flight, symbolize the rapid expansion and dominance of Babylon under Nebuchadnezzar's leadership.

Strong's Concordance: The term "eagle" (H5404 - nesher) signifies swiftness and strength, often used to describe rapid and powerful action (e.g., Exodus 19:4, Isaiah 40:31).

References: Habakkuk 1:8 - "Their horses also are swifter than leopards, and more fierce than evening wolves. Their chargers charge ahead; their cavalry comes from afar; they fly as the eagle that hastens to eat."

The Plucking of the Wings

Daniel 7:4 - "I watched till its wings were plucked off..."

Symbol: Humbling and Limitation.

Meaning: The plucking off of the wings signifies a humbling and limitation of Babylon's power and rapid expansion. This event likely refers to the period of Nebuchadnezzar's madness, as described in Daniel Chapter 4, where he was humbled by God and temporarily removed from his position of power.

References: Daniel 4:31-33 - "While the word was still in the king's mouth, a voice fell from heaven: 'King Nebuchadnezzar, to you it is spoken: the kingdom has departed from you! And they shall drive you from men, and your dwelling shall be with the beasts of the field. They shall make you eat grass like oxen; and seven times shall pass over you until you know that the Most High rules in the kingdom of men, and gives it to whomever He chooses.'"

The Transformation of the Lion

Daniel 7:4 - "...and it was lifted up from the earth and made to stand on two feet like a man, and a man's heart was given to it."

Symbol: Transformation and Humanization.

Meaning: The lifting up of the lion to stand on two feet like a man and the giving of a man's heart signify a transformation from a beastly, aggressive nature to a more humanized and compassionate state. This transformation can be seen as symbolic of Nebuchadnezzar's return to sanity and recognition of God's sovereignty, leading to a more humane and just rule.

References: Daniel 4:34-36 - "And at the end of the time, I, Nebuchadnezzar, lifted my eyes to heaven, and my understanding returned to me; and I blessed the Most High and praised and honored Him who lives forever: For His dominion is an everlasting dominion, and His kingdom is from generation to generation. All the inhabitants of the earth are reputed as nothing; He does according to His will in the army of heaven and among the inhabitants of the earth. No one can restrain His hand or say to Him, 'What have You done?' At the same time, my reason returned to me, and for the glory of my kingdom, my honor and splendor returned to me. My counselors and nobles resorted to me, I was restored to my kingdom, and excellent majesty was added to me."

Prophetic Implications

The Sovereignty of God

The vision of the lion with the eagle's wings and its subsequent transformation underscores the theme of God's sovereignty over earthly kingdoms. Despite Babylon's might and rapid conquests, God humbles the proud and raises them up according to His will. This message is consistent with the overarching theme in the Book of Daniel that God is in control of human history and the rise and fall of empires.

References: Daniel 2:21 - "And He changes the times and the seasons; He removes kings and raises up kings; He gives wisdom to the wise and knowledge to those who have understanding."

The Hope of Transformation

The transformation of the lion symbolizes the hope of redemption and change. Just as Nebuchadnezzar was transformed from a beastly ruler to a more humane and God-fearing king, this vision offers hope that even the most powerful and proud can be humbled and transformed by God's grace.

References: Ezekiel 36:26 - "I will give you a new heart and put a new spirit within you; I will take the heart of stone out of your flesh and give you a heart of flesh."

Conclusion

Daniel's vision of the lion with eagle's wings provides a profound and symbolic portrayal of the Babylonian Empire and its ruler, Nebuchadnezzar. Through the imagery of the lion and the eagle's wings, we see a depiction of Babylon's strength, rapid conquests, and eventual humbling. The transformation of the lion into a figure standing like a man with a human heart reflects the hope of redemption and the sovereignty of God over human history.

As we continue to explore the remaining beasts in Daniel Chapter 7, the insights gained from the symbolism of the lion will deepen our understanding of the broader prophetic narrative and God's ultimate control over the kingdoms of the world. The vision serves as a powerful reminder of the themes of humility, transformation, and divine sovereignty that run throughout the Book of Daniel.

CHAPTER 07

THE BEAR RAISED ON ONE SIDE: REPRESENTING THE MEO-PERSIAN EMPIRE

Daniel Chapter 7 presents a series of vivid and symbolic visions, each representing a significant kingdom in world history. In this chapter, we will focus on the second beast in Daniel's vision, the bear raised on one side, symbolizing the Medo-Persian Empire. By examining the prophetic literature, symbols, and images associated with this vision, we will offer a comprehensive commentary and interpretation, supported by Bible verses and insights from Strong's Concordance.

Daniel's Vision of the Four Beasts

Daniel 7:1-3 - "In the first year of Belshazzar king of Babylon, Daniel had a dream and visions of his head while on his bed. Then he wrote down the dream, telling the main facts. Daniel spoke, saying, 'I saw in my vision by night, and behold, the four winds of heaven were stirring up the Great Sea. And four great beasts came up from the sea, each different from the other.'"

The vision occurs during the first year of Belshazzar's reign, providing the historical context. The four winds stirring up the Great Sea symbolize the chaotic events that give rise to these powerful kingdoms.

The Second Beast: The Bear Raised on One Side

Daniel 7:5 - "And suddenly another beast, a second, like a bear. It was raised up on one side, and had three ribs in its mouth between its teeth. And they said thus to it: 'Arise, devour much flesh!'"

The Symbolism of the Bear

1. The Bear

Symbol: Medo-Persian Empire.

Meaning: The bear represents the Medo-Persian Empire, known for its strength and ferocity in conquest. Bears are powerful and formidable animals, symbolizing the empire's military prowess and dominance.

Strong's Concordance: The term "bear" (H1677 - dob) is often used to describe strength and aggressiveness, reflecting the character of the Medo-Persian Empire.

References: Isaiah 13:17-18 - "Behold, I will stir up the Medes against them, who will not regard silver; and as for gold, they will not delight in it. Also their bows will dash the young men to pieces, and they will have no pity on the fruit of the womb; their eye will not spare children."

2. Raised on One Side

Symbol: Asymmetrical Power Distribution.

Meaning: The bear being raised on one side indicates an asymmetrical power distribution within the Medo-Persian Empire. This imagery suggests that one part of the empire (Persia) was stronger and more dominant than the other part (Media).

References: Daniel 8:3 - "Then I lifted my eyes and saw, and there, standing beside the river, was a ram which had two horns, and the two horns were high; but one was higher than the other, and the higher one came up last."

The Three Ribs in Its Mouth

Daniel 7:5 - "...and had three ribs in its mouth between its teeth. And they said thus to it: 'Arise, devour much flesh!'"

Symbol: Conquests of the Medo-Persian Empire.

Meaning: The three ribs in the bear's mouth likely represent the major conquests of the Medo-Persian Empire. These could be interpreted as Babylon, Lydia, and Egypt, which were significant territories conquered by the Medo-Persians.

Strong's Concordance: The term "rib" (H6763 - tsela) is often associated with structural support, indicating the significant regions or nations that supported the empire's power.

References: Isaiah 45:1-2 - "Thus says the Lord to His anointed, to Cyrus, whose right hand I have held—to subdue nations before him and loose the armor of kings, to open before him the double doors, so that the gates will not be shut: 'I will go before you and make the crooked places straight; I will break in pieces the gates of bronze and cut the bars of iron.'"

The Command to Devour Much Flesh

Daniel 7:5 - "...And they said thus to it: 'Arise, devour much flesh!'"

Symbol: Command to Conquer.

Meaning: The command to "devour much flesh" signifies the aggressive and expansive nature of the Medo-Persian Empire. This command reflects the empire's relentless pursuit of conquest and domination over vast territories.

References: Jeremiah 51:11 - "Make the arrows bright! Gather the shields! The Lord has raised up the spirit of the kings of the Medes. For His plan is against Babylon to destroy it, because it is the vengeance of the Lord, the vengeance for His temple."

The Historical and Prophetic Context

The Medo-Persian Empire

The Medo-Persian Empire, also known as the Achaemenid Empire, was founded by Cyrus the Great around 550 B.C. after the unification of the Median and Persian tribes. The empire rapidly expanded to become one of the largest and most powerful empires in ancient history, stretching from the Balkans and Eastern Europe to the Indus Valley.

References: Ezra 1:1-2 - "Now in the first year of Cyrus king of Persia, that the word of the Lord by the mouth of Jeremiah might be fulfilled, the Lord stirred up the spirit of Cyrus king of Persia, so that he made a proclamation throughout all his kingdom, and also put it in writing, saying, 'Thus says Cyrus king of Persia: All the kingdoms of the earth the Lord God of heaven has given me. And He has commanded me to build Him a house at Jerusalem which is in Judah.'"

The Bear and the Ram: A Comparative Analysis

Daniel 8:20 - "The ram which you saw, having the two horns—they are the kings of Media and Persia."

In Daniel Chapter 8, the Medo-Persian Empire is also symbolized by a ram with two horns, one higher than the other. This vision complements the bear imagery, reinforcing the dominance of Persia over Media and highlighting the empire's significant role in biblical prophecy.

Prophetic Implications

The Sovereignty of God

The vision of the bear raised on one side emphasizes God's sovereignty over the rise and fall of empires. The Medo-Persian Empire's conquests and expansion were ultimately under God's control and served His purposes in history.

References: Daniel 2:21 - "And He changes the times and the seasons; He removes kings and raises up kings; He gives wisdom to the wise and knowledge to those who have understanding."

Divine Judgment and Deliverance

The fall of Babylon to the Medo-Persian Empire fulfilled God's judgment against Babylon and led to the deliverance of the Jewish people from exile. Cyrus the Great issued a decree allowing the Jews to return to Jerusalem and rebuild the temple, demonstrating God's faithfulness to His promises.

References: Isaiah 44:28 - "Who says of Cyrus, 'He is My shepherd, and he shall perform all My pleasure, saying to Jerusalem, "You shall be built," and to the temple, "Your foundation shall be laid."'"

Conclusion

Daniel's vision of the bear raised on one side provides a profound and symbolic portrayal of the Medo-Persian Empire. The imagery of the bear, the raised side, and the three ribs in its mouth collectively symbolize the empire's strength, asymmetrical power distribution, and significant conquests. The command to devour much flesh reflects the aggressive and expansive nature of the Medo-Persian conquests.

This vision underscores the themes of divine sovereignty, judgment, and deliverance, highlighting God's control over the course of history and His faithfulness to His people. As we continue to explore the remaining beasts in Daniel Chapter 7, the insights gained from the symbolism of the bear will deepen our understanding of the broader prophetic narrative and God's ultimate plan for the kingdoms of the world. The vision serves as a powerful reminder of the themes of divine control, judgment, and the fulfillment of God's promises throughout history.

The Leopard with Four Wings: Signifying Greece under Alexander the Great

Daniel Chapter 7 contains one of the most captivating and symbolic visions in the Bible, where Daniel sees four beasts rising from the sea, each representing a powerful kingdom. In this chapter, we will focus on the third beast, the leopard with four wings and four heads, which signifies the Greek Empire under Alexander the Great. Through a detailed analysis of the prophetic literature, symbols, and images associated with this vision, we aim to provide a comprehensive commentary and interpretation, supported by Bible verses and insights from Strong's Concordance.

Daniel's Vision of the Four Beasts

Daniel 7:1-3 - "In the first year of Belshazzar king of Babylon, Daniel had a dream and visions of his head while on his bed. Then he wrote down the dream, telling the main facts. Daniel spoke, saying, 'I saw in my vision by night, and behold, the four winds of heaven were stirring up the Great Sea. And four great beasts came up from the sea, each different from the other.'"

The vision occurs during the first year of Belshazzar's reign, providing historical context. The four winds stirring up the Great Sea symbolize the chaotic events that give rise to these powerful kingdoms.

The Third Beast: The Leopard with Four Wings and Four Heads

Daniel 7:6 - "After this I looked, and there was another, like a leopard, which had on its back four wings of a bird. The beast also had four heads, and dominion was given to it."

The Symbolism of the Leopard

1. The Leopard

Symbol: Greek Empire under Alexander the Great.

Meaning: The leopard represents the Greek Empire, known for its swiftness and agility in conquest. Leopards are fast and deadly predators, symbolizing the rapid and extensive conquests of Alexander the Great.

Strong's Concordance: The term "leopard" (H5246 - namer) is used to describe a swift and cunning predator, reflecting the nature of Alexander's military campaigns.

References: Habakkuk 1:8 - "Their horses also are swifter than leopards, and more fierce than evening wolves. Their chargers charge ahead; their cavalry comes from afar; they fly as the eagle that hastens to eat."

2. The Four Wings

Symbol: Speed and Reach of Conquests.

Meaning: The four wings on the leopard's back emphasize the exceptional speed and far-reaching conquests of Alexander the Great. Under his leadership, the Greek

Empire expanded rapidly, covering a vast territory in a short period.

Strong's Concordance: The term "wings" (H3671 - kanaph) signifies swiftness and mobility, often used to describe rapid movement and expansion.

References: Isaiah 8:8 - "He will pass through Judah, he will overflow and pass over, he will reach up to the neck; and the stretching out of his wings will fill the breadth of your land, O Immanuel."

The Four Heads of the Leopard

Daniel 7:6 - "The beast also had four heads, and dominion was given to it."

Symbol: Division of Alexander's Empire.

Meaning: The four heads of the leopard represent the division of Alexander the Great's empire into four parts after his death. His generals, known as the Diadochi, took control of different regions, leading to the establishment of four major Hellenistic kingdoms.

Strong's Concordance: The term "head" (H7218 - rosh) symbolizes leadership and authority, indicating the four rulers who succeeded Alexander.

References: Daniel 8:8 - "Therefore the male goat grew very great; but when he became strong, the large horn was broken, and in place of it four notable ones came up toward the four winds of heaven."

Historical Context of Alexander the Great

Alexander's Conquests

Alexander the Great, one of history's most renowned military leaders, created one of the largest empires in the ancient world. Born in 356 B.C., he ascended to the throne of Macedon at the age of 20 and quickly embarked on an ambitious campaign to conquer the Persian Empire. His military genius and strategic prowess enabled him to defeat much larger armies and secure vast territories from Greece to Egypt and India.

References: 1 Maccabees 1:1-4 (Apocrypha) - "After Alexander son of Philip, the Macedonian, who came from the land of Kittim, had defeated Darius, king of the Persians and the Medes, he succeeded him as king. (He had previously become king of Greece.) He fought many battles, conquered strongholds, and put to death the kings of the earth."

The Division of the Empire

After Alexander's untimely death in 323 B.C. at the age of 32, his empire was divided among his four generals: Ptolemy, Seleucus, Lysimachus, and Cassander. This division led to the formation of the Ptolemaic Kingdom in Egypt, the Seleucid Empire in Persia and Mesopotamia, the Kingdom of

Lysimachus in Thrace and Asia Minor, and the Antipatrid dynasty in Macedonia and Greece.

References: Daniel 8:22 - "As for the broken horn and the four that stood up in its place, four kingdoms shall arise out of that nation, but not with its power."

Prophetic Implications

Divine Sovereignty

The vision of the leopard with four wings and four heads emphasizes God's sovereignty over the rise and fall of empires. Despite Alexander's incredible achievements and the vastness of his empire, its division upon his death reflects the transient nature of human power and the overarching control of divine providence.

References: Daniel 2:21 - "And He changes the times and the seasons; He removes kings and raises up kings; He gives wisdom to the wise and knowledge to those who have understanding."

The Impact of Hellenization

The spread of Greek culture and language, known as Hellenization, had a profound impact on the ancient world. This cultural diffusion facilitated the spread of ideas, trade, and communication across the conquered territories, significantly influencing subsequent historical and religious developments.

References: Acts 17:28 - "For in Him we live and move and have our being, as also some of your own poets have said, 'For we are also His offspring.'"

Conclusion

Daniel's vision of the leopard with four wings and four heads provides a symbolic and prophetic portrayal of the Greek Empire under Alexander the Great. The imagery of the leopard emphasizes the speed and efficiency of Alexander's conquests, while the four wings highlight the vast reach of his empire. The four heads symbolize the division of the empire among his generals after his death.

This vision underscores the themes of divine sovereignty and the transient nature of human power, reminding us of God's ultimate control over the affairs of nations. As we continue to explore the remaining beasts in Daniel Chapter 7, the insights gained from the symbolism of the leopard will deepen our understanding of the broader prophetic narrative and God's overarching plan for the kingdoms of the world. The vision serves as a powerful reminder of the themes of divine control, the impermanence of human achievements, and the lasting impact of cultural and historical developments.

The Dreadful and Terrible Beast: Representing Rome

Daniel Chapter 7 presents a series of visions that depict the rise and fall of four great empires, each symbolized by a different beast. The fourth and final beast, described as "dreadful and terrible," represents the Roman Empire. This chapter explores the prophetic literature, symbols, and images associated with this beast, offering a comprehensive commentary and interpretation, supported by Bible verses and insights from Strong's Concordance.

Daniel's Vision of the Four Beasts

Daniel 7:1-3 - "In the first year of Belshazzar king of Babylon, Daniel had a dream and visions of his head while on his bed. Then he wrote down the dream, telling the main facts. Daniel spoke, saying, 'I saw in my vision by night, and behold, the four winds of heaven were stirring up the Great Sea. And four great beasts came up from the sea, each different from the other.'"

The vision occurs during the first year of Belshazzar's reign, providing historical context. The four winds stirring up the Great Sea symbolize the chaotic events that give rise to these powerful kingdoms.

The Fourth Beast: The Dreadful and Terrible Beast

Daniel 7:7 - "After this I saw in the night visions, and behold, a fourth beast, dreadful and terrible, exceedingly strong. It had huge iron teeth; it was devouring, breaking in pieces, and trampling the residue with its feet. It was different from all the beasts that were before it, and it had ten horns."

The Symbolism of the Dreadful and Terrible Beast

1. The Beast

Symbol: Roman Empire.

Meaning: The fourth beast represents the Roman Empire, known for its unparalleled strength, brutality, and expansive conquests. Unlike the previous beasts, this one is not likened to any specific animal, emphasizing its unique and terrifying nature.

Strong's Concordance: The term "beast" (H2423 - chayvah) indicates a wild, untamed, and often dangerous creature, reflecting the empire's fierce and ruthless character.

References: Revelation 13:1-2 - "Then I stood on the sand of the sea. And I saw a beast rising up out of the sea, having seven heads and ten horns, and on his horns ten crowns, and on his heads a blasphemous name. Now the beast which I saw was like a leopard, his feet were like the feet of a bear, and his mouth like the mouth of a lion. The dragon gave him his power, his throne, and great authority."

2. Iron Teeth

Symbol: Strength and Destructive Power.

Meaning: The huge iron teeth signify the immense strength and destructive power of the Roman Empire. Iron, a symbol of durability and strength, reflects the empire's ability to crush and break all opposition.

Strong's Concordance: The term "iron" (H6523 - parzel) denotes strength and firmness, often used to symbolize unyielding power.

References: Daniel 2:40 - "And the fourth kingdom shall be as strong as iron, inasmuch as iron breaks in pieces and shatters everything; and like iron that crushes, that kingdom will break in pieces and crush all the others."

The Beast's Actions

Daniel 7:7 - "...it was devouring, breaking in pieces, and trampling the residue with its feet."

Symbol: Conquest and Oppression.

Meaning: The actions of devouring, breaking in pieces, and trampling signify the Roman Empire's method of conquest and oppression. It subjugated and destroyed nations with brutal efficiency, leaving nothing unscathed in its wake.

References: Daniel 7:19 - "Then I wished to know the truth about the fourth beast, which was different from all the others, exceedingly dreadful, with its teeth of iron and its nails of bronze, which devoured, broke in pieces, and trampled the residue with its feet."

The Ten Horns

Daniel 7:7 - "It was different from all the beasts that were before it, and it had ten horns."

Symbol: Future Divisions of the Roman Empire.

Meaning: The ten horns represent ten kings or kingdoms that would arise from the Roman Empire. These divisions signify the fragmentation and continuation of Roman power through various successor states.

Strong's Concordance: The term "horn" (H7162 - qeren) symbolizes power and authority, often used to denote kings or leaders.

References: Daniel 7:24 - "The ten horns are ten kings who shall arise from this kingdom. And another shall rise after them; he shall be different from the first ones, and shall subdue three kings."

The Little Horn

Daniel 7:8 - "I was considering the horns, and there was another horn, a little one, coming up among them, before whom three of the first horns were plucked out by the roots. And there, in this horn, were eyes like the eyes of a man, and a mouth speaking pompous words."

Symbol: A Powerful and Arrogant Leader.

Meaning: The little horn represents a powerful and arrogant leader who would rise among the successor states of the Roman Empire. This leader is characterized by intelligence (eyes like a man) and arrogance (a mouth speaking pompous words).

Strong's Concordance: The term "little" (H2192 - ze'ir) indicates something small or insignificant in appearance but significant in influence and impact.

References: Daniel 7:25 - "He shall speak pompous words against the Most High, shall persecute the saints of the Most High, and shall intend to change times and law. Then the saints shall be given into his hand for a time and times and half a time."

Historical Context of the Roman Empire

The Rise and Expansion of Rome

The Roman Empire, founded in 27 B.C. after the end of the Roman Republic, became one of the most powerful and extensive empires in history. It reached its greatest territorial extent under Emperor Trajan in 117 A.D., controlling large parts of Europe, North Africa, and the Middle East.

References: Luke 2:1 - "And it came to pass in those days that a decree went out from Caesar Augustus that all the world should be registered."

The Division of the Empire

After centuries of dominance, the Roman Empire began to fragment in the 3rd and 4th centuries A.D. The eventual division into the Western Roman Empire and the Eastern Roman Empire (Byzantine Empire) marked the beginning of its decline. The Western Roman Empire fell in 476 A.D., while the Eastern Empire continued until the fall of Constantinople in 1453 A.D.

References: Daniel 2:41-42 - "Whereas you saw the feet and toes, partly of potter's clay and partly of iron, the kingdom shall be divided; yet the strength of the iron shall be in it, just as you saw the iron mixed with ceramic clay. And as the toes of the feet were partly of iron and partly of clay, so the kingdom shall be partly strong and partly fragile."

Prophetic Implications

The Sovereignty of God

The vision of the dreadful and terrible beast underscores the theme of God's sovereignty over the rise and fall of empires. Despite the might and brutality of the Roman Empire, its eventual decline and division were part of God's sovereign plan.

References: Daniel 4:17 - "This decision is by the decree of the watchers, and the sentence by the word of the holy ones, in order that the living may know that the Most High rules in the kingdom of men, gives it to whomever He will, and sets over it the lowest of men."

The Coming Judgment

The description of the fourth beast and its actions foreshadows the coming judgment upon oppressive and arrogant powers. The vision indicates that no matter how powerful a kingdom may be, it will ultimately be accountable to God.

References: Revelation 20:11-12 - "Then I saw a great white throne and Him who sat on it, from whose face the earth and the heaven fled away. And there was found no place for them. And I saw the dead, small and great, standing before God, and books were opened. And another book was opened, which is the Book of Life. And the dead were judged according to their works, by the things which were written in the books."

Conclusion

Daniel's vision of the dreadful and terrible beast provides a symbolic and prophetic portrayal of the Roman Empire. The imagery of the beast, its iron teeth, and its actions emphasize the strength, brutality, and expansive nature of Rome. The ten horns and the little horn signify the future divisions and the rise of powerful leaders from the remnants of the Roman Empire.

This vision underscores the themes of divine sovereignty, judgment, and the transient nature of human power, reminding us that all kingdoms and rulers are ultimately under God's control. As we continue to explore the prophetic symbols in the Book of Daniel, the insights gained from the symbolism of the fourth beast will deepen our understanding of the broader prophetic narrative and God's overarching plan for the kingdoms of the world. The vision serves as a powerful reminder of the themes of divine control, accountability, and the ultimate triumph of God's kingdom over all earthly powers.

CHAPTER 08

THE RAM WITH TWO HORNS: REPRESENTING THE MEDO-PERSIAN EMPIRE

Daniel Chapter 8 provides a detailed vision that offers significant insight into the future of two great empires: the Medo-Persian and the Greek empires. This chapter will focus exclusively on the ram with two horns, which represents the Medo-Persian Empire. By examining the prophetic literature, symbols, and images associated with this vision, we aim to provide a comprehensive commentary and interpretation, supported by Bible verses and insights from Strong's Concordance.

Daniel's Vision of the Ram and the Goat

Daniel 8:1-4 - "In the third year of the reign of King Belshazzar a vision appeared to me—to me, Daniel—after the one that appeared to me the first time. I saw in the vision, and it so happened while I was looking, that I was in Shushan, the citadel, which is in the province of Elam; and I saw in the vision that I was by the River Ulai. Then I lifted my eyes and saw, and there, standing beside the river, was a ram which had two horns, and the two horns were high, but one was higher than the other, and the higher one came up last. I saw the ram pushing westward, northward, and southward, so that no animal could withstand him; nor was there any that could deliver from his hand, but he did according to his will and became great."

The Symbolism of the Ram with Two Horns

1. The Ram

Symbol: Medo-Persian Empire.

Meaning: The ram represents the Medo-Persian Empire, known for its powerful and expansive conquests. Rams are often associated with strength and aggression, fitting symbols for this dominant empire.

Strong's Concordance: The term "ram" (H352 - 'ayil) signifies a male sheep, often used to symbolize power and leadership in biblical literature.

References: Isaiah 41:2 - "Who raised up one from the east? Who in righteousness called him to His feet? Who gave the nations before him, and made him rule over kings? Who gave them as the dust to his sword, as driven stubble to his bow?"

The Two Horns of the Ram

Daniel 8:3 - "Then I lifted my eyes and saw, and there, standing beside the river, was a ram which had two horns, and the two horns were high; but one was higher than the other, and the higher one came up last."

Symbol: Dual Kingship of Media and Persia.

Meaning: The two horns represent the dual kingship of the Medes and Persians, who together formed the Medo-Persian Empire. The fact that one horn was higher than the other and came up last indicates the dominance of Persia over Media.

Strong's Concordance: The term "horn" (H7161 - qeren) symbolizes power and authority, often used to denote kings or leaders in biblical prophecy.

References: Daniel 8:20 - "The ram which you saw, having the two horns—they are the kings of Media and Persia."

The Higher Horn Coming Up Last

Symbol: The Dominance of Persia.

Meaning: The higher horn coming up last symbolizes the rise of Persia to a dominant position within the Medo-Persian Empire. Although Media was initially prominent, Persia eventually became the more powerful and influential partner in the empire.

References: Daniel 5:28 - "PERES: Your kingdom has been divided, and given to the Medes and Persians."

The Ram's Expansion

Daniel 8:4 - "I saw the ram pushing westward, northward, and southward, so that no animal could withstand him; nor was there any that could deliver from his hand, but he did according to his will and became great."

Symbol: Conquests and Expansion.

Meaning: The ram pushing in various directions symbolizes the expansive military campaigns and conquests of the Medo-Persian Empire. The directions mentioned (westward, northward, and southward) indicate the vast extent of the empire's territorial expansion.

Strong's Concordance: The term "push" (H5055 - nagach) implies forceful movement and aggression, reflecting the empire's aggressive conquests.

References: Esther 1:1 - "Now it came to pass in the days of Ahasuerus (this was the Ahasuerus who reigned over one hundred and twenty-seven provinces, from India to Ethiopia)."

Historical Context of the Medo-Persian Empire

The Rise of Cyrus the Great

Cyrus the Great, founder of the Achaemenid Empire, played a crucial role in the rise of the Medo-Persian Empire.

In 550 B.C., he united the Medes and Persians, forming a powerful coalition that quickly expanded through military conquests. His leadership and strategic acumen allowed the empire to grow rapidly, encompassing vast territories.

References: Isaiah 45:1 - "Thus says the Lord to His anointed, to Cyrus, whose right hand I have held—to subdue nations before him and loose the armor of kings, to open before him the double doors, so that the gates will not be shut."

The Expansion of the Empire

Under Cyrus and his successors, the Medo-Persian Empire extended its reach across three continents, including parts of Europe, Africa, and Asia. Notable conquests included the defeat of Lydia, the annexation of Babylon, and the subjugation of Egypt, making it one of the largest empires in ancient history.

References: Daniel 6:28 - "So this Daniel prospered in the reign of Darius and in the reign of Cyrus the Persian."

Prophetic Implications

Divine Sovereignty

The vision of the ram with two horns underscores the theme of God's sovereignty over the rise and fall of empires. Despite the power and might of the Medo-Persian Empire, its success and expansion were ultimately under God's control and served His purposes in history.

References: Daniel 2:21 - "And He changes the times and the seasons; He removes kings and raises up kings; He gives wisdom to the wise and knowledge to those who have understanding."

Fulfillment of Prophecy

The Medo-Persian Empire's conquests and dominance fulfilled several biblical prophecies. Isaiah and Jeremiah had prophesied the rise of a power from the east that would conquer Babylon and liberate the Jewish exiles, which was accomplished under Cyrus the Great.

References: Jeremiah 51:11 - "Make the arrows bright! Gather the shields! The Lord has raised up the spirit of the kings of the Medes. For His plan is against Babylon to destroy it, because it is the vengeance of the Lord, the vengeance for His temple."

Conclusion

Daniel's vision of the ram with two horns provides a symbolic and prophetic portrayal of the Medo-Persian Empire. The imagery of the ram and its two horns emphasizes the dual kingship of Media and Persia, with Persia eventually becoming the dominant power. The ram's aggressive expansion in various directions symbolizes the vast territorial conquests of the empire.

This vision underscores the themes of divine sovereignty and the fulfillment of prophecy, highlighting God's control over the rise and fall of empires. As we continue to explore the prophetic symbols in the Book of Daniel, the insights gained from the symbolism of the ram will deepen our understanding of the broader prophetic narrative and God's overarching plan for the kingdoms of the world. The vision serves as a powerful reminder of the themes of divine control, the impermanence of human power, and the fulfillment of God's promises throughout history.

The Goat with a Prominent Horn: Symbolizing Greece under Alexander the Great

Daniel Chapter 8 presents a detailed vision that significantly outlines the future of two great empires: the Medo-Persian and the Greek empires. This chapter will focus on the goat with a prominent horn, which symbolizes the Greek Empire under Alexander the Great. By examining the prophetic literature, symbols, and images associated with this vision, we aim to provide a comprehensive commentary and interpretation, supported by Bible verses and insights from Strong's Concordance.

Daniel's Vision of the Ram and the Goat

Daniel 8:1-5 - "In the third year of the reign of King Belshazzar a vision appeared to me—to me, Daniel—after the one that appeared to me the first time. I saw in the vision, and it so happened while I was looking, that I was in Shushan, the citadel, which is in the province of Elam; and I saw in the vision that I was by the River Ulai. Then I lifted my eyes and saw, and there, standing beside the river, was a ram which had two horns, and the two horns were high; but one was higher than the other, and the higher one came up last. I saw the ram pushing westward, northward, and southward, so that no animal could withstand him; nor was there any that could deliver from his hand, but he did according to his will and became great. And as I was considering, suddenly a male goat came from the west, across the surface of the whole earth, without touching the ground; and the goat had a notable horn between his eyes."

The Symbolism of the Goat with a Prominent Horn

1. The Goat

Symbol: Greek Empire.

Meaning: The goat represents the Greek Empire, known for its agility, speed, and the rapid expansion of its territory under Alexander the Great. Goats are often associated with agility and swiftness, fitting symbols for Alexander's military campaigns.

Strong's Concordance: The term "goat" (H6842 - tsaphir) signifies a male goat, often used to symbolize leadership and aggression in biblical literature.

References: Daniel 8:21 - "And the male goat is the kingdom of Greece. The large horn that is between its eyes is the first king."

2. The Prominent Horn

Symbol: Alexander the Great.

Meaning: The prominent horn on the goat represents Alexander the Great, the first king of the Greek Empire. The notable horn signifies his exceptional leadership and the significant impact of his conquests.

Strong's Concordance: The term "horn" (H7161 - qeren) symbolizes power and authority, often used to denote kings or leaders in biblical prophecy.

References: Daniel 8:5 - "...and the goat had a notable horn between his eyes."

The Goat's Actions

Daniel 8:6-7 - "Then he came to the ram that had two horns, which I had seen standing beside the river, and ran at him with furious power. And I saw him confronting the ram; he was moved with rage against him, attacked the ram, and broke his two horns. There was no power in the ram to withstand him, but he cast him down to the ground and trampled him; and there was no one that could deliver the ram from his hand."

Symbol: Conquest of the Medo-Persian Empire.

Meaning: The goat's attack on the ram symbolizes Alexander the Great's conquest of the Medo-Persian Empire. The breaking of the ram's two horns signifies the defeat of the dual kingship of Media and Persia, establishing Greek dominance.

Strong's Concordance: The term "rage" (H2534 - chemah) indicates intense anger or wrath, reflecting the intensity and decisiveness of Alexander's military campaigns.

References: Daniel 8:20-21 - "The ram which you saw, having the two horns—they are the kings of Media and Persia. And the male goat is the kingdom of Greece. The large horn that is between its eyes is the first king."

The Speed of the Goat

Daniel 8:5 - "...suddenly a male goat came from the west, across the surface of the whole earth, without touching the ground..."

Symbol: Rapid Conquests.

Meaning: The description of the goat moving across the earth without touching the ground signifies the unprecedented speed and efficiency of Alexander the Great's military campaigns. His conquests were swift, covering vast territories in a short period.

Strong's Concordance: The term "without touching the ground" (H3802 - magar) emphasizes speed and agility, reflecting the rapid movement of Alexander's army.

References: Habakkuk 1:8 - "Their horses also are swifter than leopards, and more fierce than evening wolves. Their chargers charge ahead; their cavalry comes from afar; they fly as the eagle that hastens to eat."

The Breaking of the Prominent Horn

Daniel 8:8 - "Therefore the male goat grew very great; but when he became strong, the large horn was broken, and in place of it four notable ones came up toward the four winds of heaven."

Symbol: Death of Alexander the Great.

Meaning: The breaking of the prominent horn represents the untimely death of Alexander the Great at the height of his power. Despite his great conquests and achievements, his empire did not remain united after his death.

Strong's Concordance: The term "broken" (H7665 - shabar) indicates a sudden and forceful break, reflecting the unexpected end of Alexander's rule.

References: Daniel 11:4 - "And when he has arisen, his kingdom shall be broken up and divided toward the four winds of heaven, but not among his posterity nor according to his dominion with which he ruled; for his kingdom shall be uprooted, even for others besides these."

The Four Successor Horns

Daniel 8:8 - "...and in place of it four notable ones came up toward the four winds of heaven."

Symbol: Division of Alexander's Empire.

Meaning: The four notable horns that replace the broken horn symbolize the division of Alexander's empire among his four generals, known as the Diadochi. This division led to the formation of four major Hellenistic kingdoms: the Ptolemaic Kingdom in Egypt, the Seleucid Empire in Persia and Mesopotamia, the Kingdom of Lysimachus in Thrace and Asia Minor, and the Antipatrid dynasty in Macedonia and Greece.

Strong's Concordance: The term "notable" (H117 - 'addiyr) signifies something prominent or excellent, indicating the significant status of the four successor kingdoms.

References: Daniel 8:22 - "As for the broken horn and the four that stood up in its place, four kingdoms shall arise out of that nation, but not with its power."

Historical Context of Alexander the Great

The Rise of Alexander

Alexander the Great, born in 356 B.C., became king of Macedon in 336 B.C. after the assassination of his father, King Philip II. He swiftly consolidated his power and embarked on an ambitious campaign to conquer the Persian Empire. Within a decade, Alexander created one of the largest empires in history, stretching from Greece to Egypt and into northwest India.

References: 1 Maccabees 1:1-4 (Apocrypha) - "After Alexander son of Philip, the Macedonian, who came from the land of Kittim, had defeated Darius, king of the Persians and the Medes, he succeeded him as king. (He had previously become king of Greece.) He fought many battles, conquered strongholds, and put to death the kings of the earth."

The Division of the Empire

Following Alexander's death in 323 B.C. at the age of 32, his empire was divided among his generals, leading to the creation of several Hellenistic states. These divisions marked the end of unified Greek control and set the stage for centuries of conflict and power struggles among the successor kingdoms.

References: Daniel 8:22 - "As for the broken horn and the four that stood up in its place, four kingdoms shall arise out of that nation, but not with its power."

Prophetic Implications

Divine Sovereignty

The vision of the goat with a prominent horn emphasizes God's sovereignty over the rise and fall of empires. Despite Alexander's remarkable achievements and the vastness of his empire, its sudden division after his death reflects the transient nature of human power and the overarching control of divine providence.

References: Daniel 2:21 - "And He changes the times and the seasons; He removes kings and raises up kings; He gives wisdom to the wise and knowledge to those who have understanding."

The Spread of Hellenism

Alexander's conquests facilitated the spread of Greek culture and language, a process known as Hellenization. This cultural diffusion had profound implications for the ancient world, influencing subsequent historical and religious developments, including the context of the New Testament.

References: Acts 17:28 - "For in Him we live and move and have our being, as also some of your own poets have said, 'For we are also His offspring.'"

Conclusion

Daniel's vision of the goat with a prominent horn provides a symbolic and prophetic portrayal of the Greek

Empire under Alexander the Great. The imagery of the goat and its notable horn emphasizes the rapid and extensive conquests of Alexander, while the breaking of the horn signifies his untimely death and the subsequent division of his empire.

This vision underscores the themes of divine sovereignty and the transient nature of human power, reminding us that all kingdoms and rulers are ultimately under God's control. As we continue to explore the prophetic symbols in the Book of Daniel, the insights gained from the symbolism of the goat will deepen our understanding of the broader prophetic narrative and God's overarching plan for the kingdoms of the world. The vision serves as a powerful reminder of the themes of divine control, the impermanence of human achievements, and the lasting impact of cultural and historical developments.

The Broken Horn and the Four Successor Horns: Depicting the Division of Alexander's Empire

Daniel Chapter 8 provides a vivid prophetic vision concerning the future of great empires. Following the symbolism of the goat with a prominent horn representing the Greek Empire under Alexander the Great, this chapter will focus on the broken horn and the four successor horns, which depict the division of Alexander's empire after his death. By examining the prophetic literature, symbols, and images associated with this vision, we aim to provide a comprehensive commentary and interpretation, supported by Bible verses and insights from Strong's Concordance.

The Vision of the Broken Horn and the Four Successor Horns

Daniel 8:8 - "Therefore the male goat grew very great; but when he became strong, the large horn was broken, and in place of it four notable ones came up toward the four winds of heaven."

The Broken Horn

Symbolism of the Broken Horn

Symbol: The Death of Alexander the Great.

Meaning: The breaking of the prominent horn represents the untimely death of Alexander the Great at the height of his power. Despite his extensive conquests and achievements, Alexander's empire did not remain united after his death.

Strong's Concordance: The term "broken" (H7665 - shabar) indicates a sudden and forceful break, reflecting the unexpected end of Alexander's rule.

References: Daniel 11:4 - "And when he has arisen, his kingdom shall be broken up and divided toward the four winds of heaven, but not among his posterity nor according to his dominion with which he ruled; for his kingdom shall be uprooted, even for others besides these."

Historical Context of Alexander's Death

Alexander the Great died in 323 B.C. at the age of 32 in Babylon, under mysterious circumstances. His death left a power vacuum, as he had not established a clear succession plan. The absence of a strong heir led to the fragmentation of his vast empire.

References: 1 Maccabees 1:1-2 (Apocrypha) - "After Alexander son of Philip, the Macedonian, who came from the land of Kittim, had defeated Darius, king of the Persians and the Medes, he succeeded him as king. He had previously become king of Greece."

The Four Successor Horns

Daniel 8:8 - "...and in place of it four notable ones came up toward the four winds of heaven."

Symbolism of the Four Successor Horns

Symbol: The Division of Alexander's Empire.

Meaning: The four notable horns that replace the broken horn symbolize the division of Alexander's empire among his four generals, known as the Diadochi. This division resulted in the formation of four major Hellenistic kingdoms.

Strong's Concordance: The term "notable" (H117 - 'addiyr) signifies something prominent or excellent, indicating the significant status of the four successor kingdoms.

References: Daniel 8:22 - "As for the broken horn and the four that stood up in its place, four kingdoms shall arise out of that nation, but not with its power."

Historical Context of the Division

After Alexander's death, his empire was eventually divided among his top generals during the Wars of the Diadochi. The main divisions were:

1. Ptolemaic Kingdom (Egypt):

    - General: Ptolemy I Soter

    - Region: Egypt and parts of the Levant.

    - Significance: The Ptolemaic Kingdom became a significant cultural and economic center, with Alexandria as a prominent city.

References: Daniel 11:5 - "Also the king of the South shall become strong, as well as one of his princes; and he shall gain power over him and have dominion. His dominion shall be a great dominion."

2. Seleucid Empire (Syria and Mesopotamia):

    - General: Seleucus I Nicator

    - Region: Mesopotamia, Persia, and parts of Asia Minor.

- Significance: The Seleucid Empire was known for its vast territory and frequent conflicts with the Ptolemaic Kingdom.

References: Daniel 11:6 - "And at the end of some years they shall join forces, for the daughter of the king of the South shall go to the king of the North to make an agreement; but she shall not retain the power of her authority, and neither he nor his authority shall stand; but she shall be given up, with those who brought her, and with him who begot her and with him who strengthened her in those times."

3. Kingdom of Lysimachus (Thrace and Asia Minor):

- General: Lysimachus

- Region: Thrace and western Asia Minor.

- Significance: This kingdom was smaller and less influential compared to the Ptolemaic and Seleucid empires.

References: Daniel 8:22 - "As for the broken horn and the four that stood up in its place, four kingdoms shall arise out of that nation, but not with its power."

4. Antigonid Dynasty (Macedonia and Greece):

- General: Antigonus I Monophthalmus and later his descendants.

- Region: Macedonia and parts of Greece.

- Significance: The Antigonid Dynasty maintained control over Greece and Macedonia, frequently engaging in conflicts with the other successor states.

References: Daniel 8:9 - "And out of one of them came a little horn which grew exceedingly great toward the south, toward the east, and toward the Glorious Land."

Prophetic Implications

The Transient Nature of Human Empires

The division of Alexander's empire underscores the transient nature of human power and the futility of earthly conquests. Despite Alexander's unparalleled achievements, his empire quickly fragmented after his death, highlighting the impermanence of human endeavors.

References: Ecclesiastes 1:2 - "Vanity of vanities, says the Preacher; vanity of vanities, all is vanity."

Divine Sovereignty

The vision of the broken horn and the four successor horns emphasizes God's sovereignty over the rise and fall of empires. The division of Alexander's empire was not a mere historical accident but a fulfillment of divine prophecy, demonstrating God's control over the course of history.

References: Daniel 2:21 - "And He changes the times and the seasons; He removes kings and raises up kings; He gives wisdom to the wise and knowledge to those who have understanding."

Conclusion

Daniel's vision of the broken horn and the four successor horns provides a symbolic and prophetic portrayal of the division of Alexander the Great's empire. The imagery of the broken horn signifies Alexander's untimely death, while the four notable horns represent the subsequent division of his empire among his generals.

This vision underscores the themes of divine sovereignty and the transient nature of human power, reminding us that all kingdoms and rulers are ultimately under God's control. As we continue to explore the prophetic symbols in the Book of Daniel, the insights gained from the symbolism of the broken horn and the four successor horns will deepen our understanding of the broader prophetic narrative and God's overarching plan for the kingdoms of the world. The vision serves as a powerful reminder of the themes of divine control, the impermanence of human achievements, and the fulfillment of God's promises throughout history.

CHAPTER 09

THE HISTORICAL CONTEXT OF THE SEVENTY WEEKS PROPHECY (DANIEL 9)

The prophecy of the seventy weeks in Daniel Chapter 9 is a cornerstone of biblical eschatology and one of the most debated and analyzed prophecies in the Bible. To fully understand its significance, it is crucial to explore the historical context in which this prophecy was given. This chapter delves into the historical backdrop of the seventy weeks, examining the socio-political, religious, and cultural conditions of the time.

The Setting of Daniel's Prayer and Prophecy

Daniel 9:1-3 - "In the first year of Darius the son of Ahasuerus, of the lineage of the Medes, who was made king over the realm of the Chaldeans—in the first year of his reign I, Daniel, understood by the books the number of the years specified by the word of the Lord through Jeremiah the prophet, that He would accomplish seventy years in the desolations of Jerusalem. Then I set my face toward the Lord God to make request by prayer and supplications, with fasting, sackcloth, and ashes."

The Reign of Darius the Mede

The prophecy occurs in the first year of Darius the Mede's reign over Babylon, following the conquest of the Babylonian Empire by the Medo-Persian Empire in 539 B.C. Darius, identified as the son of Ahasuerus (Xerxes), ruled as a vassal king under Cyrus the Great. This period marks a significant transition in the region, with the fall of Babylon and the rise of the Medo-Persian Empire, which would play a crucial role in the fulfillment of the seventy-week prophecy.

References: Daniel 5:31 - "And Darius the Mede received the kingdom, being about sixty-two years old."

The Babylonian Exile and Its Impact

The Captivity of Judah

The Babylonian exile, also known as the Babylonian captivity, was a period during which the people of Judah were taken captive by Babylon. This event occurred in several waves, beginning in 605 B.C. with the first deportation, followed by subsequent deportations in 597 B.C. and 586 B.C., culminating in the destruction of Jerusalem and the

Temple. The exile was a result of Judah's persistent idolatry, disobedience, and failure to heed the warnings of the prophets.

References: 2 Kings 25:1-21 - "In the ninth year of Zedekiah's reign, on the tenth day of the tenth month, Nebuchadnezzar king of Babylon marched against Jerusalem with his whole army. He encamped outside the city and built siege works all around it. The city was kept under siege until the eleventh year of King Zedekiah."

The Prophecy of Jeremiah

The prophet Jeremiah had prophesied that the Babylonian captivity would last seventy years, a period during which the land of Judah would enjoy its sabbath rests. This seventy-year period was a key element in Daniel's prayer and understanding of the timing for the restoration of Jerusalem.

References: Jeremiah 25:11-12 - "And this whole land shall be a desolation and an astonishment, and these nations shall serve the king of Babylon seventy years. Then it will come to pass, when seventy years are completed, that I will punish the king of Babylon and that nation, the land of the Chaldeans, for their iniquity, says the Lord; and I will make it a perpetual desolation."

The Return from Exile

The Decree of Cyrus

In 539 B.C., Cyrus the Great conquered Babylon and issued a decree allowing the Jewish exiles to return to their homeland and rebuild the Temple. This decree marked the beginning of the fulfillment of Jeremiah's prophecy and set the stage for the seventy-week prophecy given to Daniel.

References: Ezra 1:1-3 - "Now in the first year of Cyrus king of Persia, that the word of the Lord by the mouth of Jeremiah might be fulfilled, the Lord stirred up the spirit of Cyrus king of Persia, so that he made a proclamation throughout all his kingdom, and also put it in writing, saying, 'Thus says Cyrus king of Persia: All the kingdoms of the earth the Lord God of heaven has given me. And He has commanded me to build Him a house at Jerusalem which is in Judah. Who is among you of all His people? May his God be with him, and let him go up to Jerusalem which is in Judah, and build the house of the Lord God of Israel (He is God), which is in Jerusalem.'"

The Rebuilding of Jerusalem and the Temple

The return from exile was a pivotal moment in Jewish history, leading to the rebuilding of Jerusalem and the Second Temple. Under the leadership of figures such as Zerubbabel, Joshua the High Priest, Ezra, and Nehemiah, the exiles worked to restore the city and reinstate the worship of Yahweh.

References: Nehemiah 2:17-18 - "Then I said to them, 'You see the distress that we are in, how Jerusalem lies waste, and its gates are burned with fire. Come and let us build the wall of Jerusalem, that we may no longer be a reproach.' And I told them of the hand of my God which had been good upon me, and also of the king's words that he had spoken to me. So they said, 'Let us rise up and build.' Then they set their hands to this good work."

Daniel's Prayer and Confession

Daniel 9:4-19 - Daniel's prayer of confession and supplication is a heartfelt plea for God's mercy and forgiveness. He acknowledges the sins of Israel and appeals to God's covenant faithfulness and compassion.

The Content of Daniel's Prayer

Daniel's prayer includes several key elements:

1. Confession of Sin: Daniel acknowledges the sins of the people, their rebellion against God's commandments, and their failure to listen to the prophets.

References: Daniel 9:5-6 - "We have sinned and committed iniquity, we have done wickedly and rebelled, even by departing from Your precepts and Your judgments. Neither have we heeded Your servants the prophets, who spoke in Your name to our kings and our princes, to our fathers and all the people of the land."

2. Appeal to God's Mercy: Daniel appeals to God's great mercy and compassion, asking Him to turn away His wrath and restore Jerusalem for the sake of His name.

References: Daniel 9:18-19 - "O my God, incline Your ear and hear; open Your eyes and see our desolations, and the city which is called by Your name; for we do not present our supplications before You because of our righteous deeds, but because of Your great mercies. O Lord, hear! O Lord, forgive! O Lord, listen and act! Do not delay for Your own sake, my God, for Your city and Your people are called by Your name."

3. Covenant Faithfulness: Daniel appeals to God's covenant faithfulness, reminding Him of His promises to His people and His commitment to Jerusalem.

References: Daniel 9:4 - "And I prayed to the Lord my God, and made confession, and said, 'O Lord, great and awesome God, who keeps His covenant and mercy with those who love Him, and with those who keep His commandments.'"

The Angelic Response

Daniel 9:20-23 - While Daniel was praying, the angel Gabriel appeared to him, providing a response from God. Gabriel's message included the prophecy of the seventy weeks, which outlined God's plan for the restoration and ultimate redemption of Israel.

References: Daniel 9:21-23 - "Yes, while I was speaking in prayer, the man Gabriel, whom I had seen in the vision at the beginning, being caused to fly swiftly, reached me about the time of the evening offering. And he informed me and talked with me, and said, 'O Daniel, I have now come forth to give you the skill to understand. At the beginning of your supplications, the command went out, and I have come to tell you, for you are greatly beloved; therefore consider the matter, and understand the vision.'"

The Seventy Weeks Prophecy

Daniel 9:24-27 - The prophecy of the seventy weeks is a complex and detailed revelation concerning the future of Israel, the coming of the Messiah, and the ultimate establishment of God's kingdom.

The Purpose of the Seventy Weeks

Daniel 9:24 - "Seventy weeks are determined for your people and for your holy city, to finish the transgression, to make an end of sins, to make reconciliation for iniquity, to bring in everlasting righteousness, to seal up vision and prophecy, and to anoint the Most Holy."

Historical Significance

The seventy weeks prophecy outlines a timeline for the fulfillment of key events in God's redemptive plan, including the coming of the Messiah, the atonement for sin, and the establishment of everlasting righteousness. This prophecy provides a framework for understanding the unfolding of God's plan for Israel and the world.

References: Luke 24:44 - "Then He said to them, 'These are the words which I spoke to you while I was still with you, that all things must be fulfilled which were written in the Law of Moses and the Prophets and the Psalms concerning Me.'"

Conclusion

The historical context of the seventy-week prophecy is essential for understanding its significance and implications. The period of the Babylonian exile, the decree of Cyrus, the rebuilding of Jerusalem, and Daniel's fervent prayer all set the stage for this remarkable prophecy. As we delve deeper into the specifics of the seventy weeks, this historical backdrop provides the foundation for comprehending the profound revelations given to Daniel and their relevance for biblical eschatology.

The seventy-week prophecy serves as a powerful reminder of God's sovereignty, faithfulness, and redemptive plan for humanity. Through the lens of history, we see the intricate workings of divine providence, guiding the course of nations and fulfilling His promises to His people.

CHAPTER 10

THE BREAKDOWN OF THE SEVENTY WEEKS: SEVEN WEEKS, SIXTY-TWO WEEKS, AND THE FINAL WEEK

The prophecy of the seventy weeks in Daniel 9:24-27 is a cornerstone of biblical eschatology, providing a detailed timeline of significant events in God's redemptive plan for Israel and the world. This chapter focuses on breaking down the seventy weeks into its three distinct periods: seven weeks, sixty-two weeks, and the final week. By examining these divisions in detail, we aim to offer a comprehensive understanding of their significance and prophetic implications, supported by Bible verses and insights from Strong's Concordance.

The Seventy Weeks Prophecy

Daniel 9:24-27 - "Seventy weeks are determined for your people and for your holy city, to finish the transgression, to make an end of sins, to make reconciliation for iniquity, to bring in everlasting righteousness, to seal up vision and prophecy, and to anoint the Most Holy. Know therefore and understand, that from the going forth of the command to restore and build Jerusalem until Messiah the Prince, there shall be seven weeks and sixty-two weeks; the street shall be built again, and the wall, even in troublesome times. And after the sixty-two weeks Messiah shall be cut off, but not for Himself; and the people of the prince who is to come shall destroy the city and the sanctuary. The end of it shall be with a flood, and till the end of the war desolations are determined. Then he shall confirm a covenant with many for one week; but in the middle of the week, he shall bring an end to sacrifice and offering. And on the wing of abominations shall be one who makes desolate, even until the consummation, which is determined, is poured out on the desolate."

The Breakdown of the Seventy Weeks

The Seven Weeks

Daniel 9:25 - "Know therefore and understand, that from the going forth of the command to restore and build Jerusalem until Messiah the Prince, there shall be seven weeks and sixty-two weeks; the street shall be built again, and the wall, even in troublesome times."

1. The Command to Restore and Build Jerusalem

Historical Context: The starting point of the seventy weeks is marked by the command to restore and build Jerusalem. This decree was issued by Persian King Artaxerxes in 445 B.C., allowing Nehemiah to return and rebuild the walls of Jerusalem.

References: Nehemiah 2:1-8 - "And it came to pass in the month of Nisan, in the twentieth year of King Artaxerxes, when wine was before him, that I took the wine and gave it to the king. Now I had never been sad in his presence before. Therefore the king said to me, 'Why is your face sad, since you are not sick? This is nothing but sorrow of heart.' So I became dreadfully afraid, and said to the king, 'May the king live forever! Why should my face not be sad, when the city, the place of my fathers' tombs, lies waste, and its gates are burned with fire?' Then the king said to me, 'What do you request?' So I prayed to the God of heaven. And I said to the king, 'If it pleases the king, and if your servant has found favor in your sight, I ask that you send me to Judah, to the city of my fathers' tombs, that I may rebuild it.' Then the king said to me (the queen also sitting beside him), 'How long will your journey be? And when will you return?' So it pleased the king to send me; and I set him a time. Furthermore I said to the king, 'If it pleases the king, let letters be given to me for the governors of the region beyond the River, that they must permit me to pass through till I come to Judah, and a letter to Asaph the keeper of the king's forest, that he must give me timber to make beams for the gates of the citadel which pertains to the temple, for the city wall, and for the house that I will occupy.' And the king granted them to me according to the good hand of my God upon me."

2. The Duration and Significance

Symbolism: The seven weeks (49 years) represent the initial period of restoration and rebuilding of Jerusalem, including the streets and the walls, even amidst opposition and challenging circumstances.

Historical Fulfillment: This period covers the time from the decree in 445 B.C. to the completion of the restoration efforts, including the rebuilding of the walls under Nehemiah and the re-establishment of the city's infrastructure.

References: Nehemiah 6:15-16 - "So the wall was finished on the twenty-fifth day of Elul, in fifty-two days. And it happened, when all our enemies heard of it, and all the nations around us saw these things, that they were very disheartened in their own eyes; for they perceived that this work was done by our God."

The Sixty-Two Weeks

Daniel 9:25-26 - "...until Messiah the Prince, there shall be seven weeks and sixty-two weeks... And after the sixty-two weeks Messiah shall be cut off, but not for Himself; and the people of the prince who is to come shall destroy the city and the sanctuary. The end of it shall be with a flood, and till the end of the war desolations are determined."

1. The Duration and Significance

Symbolism: The sixty-two weeks (434 years) extend from the completion of the restoration of Jerusalem to the coming of Messiah the Prince. This period encompasses the intertestamental period and the time leading up to the ministry of Jesus Christ.

Historical Fulfillment: This period concludes with the arrival of Jesus, who is recognized as the Messiah. The term "cut off" refers to His crucifixion, indicating that He would be rejected and killed, not for His own sins but for the sins of humanity.

References: Isaiah 53:8 - "He was taken from prison and from judgment, and who will declare His generation? For He was cut off from the land of the living; for the transgressions of My people He was stricken."

2. The Destruction of Jerusalem

Symbolism: The prophecy also foretells the destruction of Jerusalem and the Temple by the people of the prince who is to come. This refers to the Roman destruction of Jerusalem in 70 A.D.

Historical Fulfillment: In 70 A.D., the Roman general Titus led the siege of Jerusalem, resulting in the city's destruction and the Temple being set on fire and demolished, fulfilling the prophecy's prediction of desolation.

References: Matthew 24:2 - "And Jesus said to them, 'Do you not see all these things? Assuredly, I say to you, not one stone shall be left here upon another, that shall not be thrown down.'"

The Final Week

Daniel 9:27 - "Then he shall confirm a covenant with many for one week; but in the middle of the week he shall bring an end to sacrifice and offering. And on the wing of abominations shall be one who makes desolate, even until the consummation, which is determined, is poured out on the desolate."

1. The Duration and Significance

Symbolism: The final week (seven years) is often interpreted as a future period, separate from the previous sixty-nine weeks. This week is divided into two halves, with significant events occurring in the middle.

Interpretation: This period is commonly associated with the end times and the events described in the Book of Revelation. It involves a covenant being confirmed with many, an interruption of temple sacrifices, and the rise of an abominable figure who brings desolation.

References: Revelation 13:5-7 - "And he was given a mouth speaking great things and blasphemies, and he was given authority to continue for forty-two months. Then he opened his mouth in blasphemy against God, to blaspheme His name, His tabernacle, and those who dwell in heaven. It was granted to him to make war with the saints and to overcome them. And authority was given him over every tribe, tongue, and nation."

2. The Covenant and Abominations

Symbolism: The confirmation of a covenant and the cessation of sacrifices in the middle of the week are significant events that indicate a breach of divine order and the rise of sacrilege.

Interpretation: The figure who confirms the covenant is often identified with the Antichrist, who will deceive many and cause great tribulation. The "abomination of desolation" refers to acts of profound disrespect and desecration of holy places.

References: Matthew 24:15 - "Therefore when you see the 'abomination of desolation,' spoken of by Daniel the prophet, standing in the holy place (whoever reads, let him understand)."

Conclusion

The breakdown of the seventy weeks prophecy in Daniel 9 provides a detailed and profound timeline of significant events in God's redemptive plan. The initial seven weeks focus on the restoration and rebuilding of Jerusalem, the sixty-two weeks lead to the coming of the Messiah and His crucifixion and the final week points to future events involving end-times prophecy.

Understanding these divisions helps us to see the meticulous fulfillment of prophecy throughout history and offers insight into future events as foretold in the Scriptures. The seventy-week prophecy underscores the themes of divine sovereignty, the fulfillment of God's promises, and the ultimate establishment of His kingdom. Through this prophetic timeline, we are reminded of God's control over history and His unwavering commitment to His redemptive plan for humanity.

CHAPTER 11

THE ANOINTED ONE AND THE COVENANT

The prophecy of the seventy weeks in Daniel 9:24-27 is a profound and detailed revelation of God's plan for Israel and the world. Central to this prophecy are the figures of the Anointed One (Messiah) and the covenant. This chapter focuses on the Anointed One and the covenant, exploring their significance and implications within the context of the seventy-week prophecy. By examining these elements in detail, we aim to offer a comprehensive understanding supported by Bible verses and insights from Strong's Concordance.

The Anointed One

Daniel 9:25-26 - "Know therefore and understand, that from the going forth of the command to restore and build

Jerusalem until Messiah the Prince, there shall be seven weeks and sixty-two weeks; the street shall be built again, and the wall, even in troublesome times. And after the sixty-two weeks Messiah shall be cut off, but not for Himself; and the people of the prince who is to come shall destroy the city and the sanctuary. The end of it shall be with a flood, and till the end of the war desolations are determined."

Identification of the Anointed One

1. The Title "Messiah the Prince"

Symbolism: The title "Messiah the Prince" (H4899 - mashiach nagiyd) combines the concept of an anointed one with that of a ruling leader. The term "Messiah" means "anointed one," while "Prince" denotes a leader or ruler.

References: Psalm 2:2 - "The kings of the earth set themselves, and the rulers take counsel together, against the Lord and against His Anointed, saying..."

2. Historical Fulfillment

Interpretation: The Anointed One is identified as Jesus Christ, who is recognized as the Messiah in Christian theology. His arrival corresponds to the conclusion of the sixty-nine weeks (seven weeks plus sixty-two weeks) from the decree to restore and rebuild Jerusalem.

References: Luke 3:21-22 - "When all the people were baptized, it came to pass that Jesus also was baptized; and while He prayed, the heaven was opened. And the Holy Spirit descended in bodily form like a dove upon Him, and a voice came from heaven which said, 'You are My beloved Son; in You I am well pleased.'"

The Cutting Off of the Messiah

Daniel 9:26 - "And after the sixty-two weeks Messiah shall be cut off, but not for Himself..."

1. The Phrase "Cut Off"

Symbolism: The phrase "cut off" (H3772 - karath) signifies a violent and untimely death. This term is often used to describe a person being removed or killed.

References: Isaiah 53:8 - "He was taken from prison and from judgment, and who will declare His generation? For He was cut off from the land of the living; for the transgressions of My people He was stricken."

2. The Purpose of His Death

Interpretation: The Messiah's death is understood as an atoning sacrifice for the sins of humanity. He was "cut off" not for His own sins, but for the sins of others, fulfilling the prophecies of a suffering servant.

References: 1 Peter 3:18 - "For Christ also suffered once for sins, the just for the unjust, that He might bring us to God, being put to death in the flesh but made alive by the Spirit."

The Covenant

Daniel 9:27 - "Then he shall confirm a covenant with many for one week, but in the middle of the week he shall bring an end to sacrifice and offering. And on the wing of abominations shall be one who makes desolate, even until the consummation, which is determined, is poured out on the desolate."

The Confirmation of the Covenant

1. The Covenant

Symbolism: The term "covenant" (H1285 - berith) refers to a solemn agreement or promise. In biblical terms, covenants often represent significant commitments between God and humanity or between individuals.

References: Genesis 17:7 - "And I will establish My covenant between Me and you and your descendants after you in their generations, for an everlasting covenant, to be God to you and your descendants after you."

2. The Figure Confirming the Covenant

Interpretation: The identity of the figure who confirms the covenant is debated among scholars. Some interpret this figure as the Messiah, who establishes a new covenant through His sacrifice. Others view this figure as a future ruler (often identified with the Antichrist) who makes a deceptive covenant with many.

References: Hebrews 9:15 - "And for this reason He is the Mediator of the new covenant, by means of death, for the redemption of the transgressions under the first covenant, that those who are called may receive the promise of the eternal inheritance."

The Termination of Sacrifice and Offering

1. The Middle of the Week

Symbolism: The phrase "in the middle of the week" indicates a significant event occurring halfway through the final seven-year period (three and a half years). This event is associated with the cessation of regular temple sacrifices.

References: Daniel 12:11 - "And from the time that the daily sacrifice is taken away, and the abomination of desolation is set up, there shall be one thousand two hundred and ninety days."

2. The End of Sacrifice and Offering

Interpretation: The termination of sacrifice and offering can be seen in two ways. One interpretation is that it refers to the sacrificial system ending with the Messiah's atoning death, rendering the temple sacrifices obsolete. Another interpretation associates it with a future cessation of temple sacrifices by an oppressive ruler.

References: Hebrews 10:10-12 - "By that will we have been sanctified through the offering of the body of Jesus

Christ once for all. And every priest stands ministering daily and offering repeatedly the same sacrifices, which can never take away sins. But this Man, after He had offered one sacrifice for sins forever, sat down at the right hand of God."

The Abomination of Desolation

Daniel 9:27 - "And on the wing of abominations shall be one who makes desolate, even until the consummation, which is determined, is poured out on the desolate."

The Term "Abomination"

Symbolism: The term "abomination" (H8251 - shiqquwts) refers to something detestable or repulsive, often associated with idolatry and sacrilege in the Bible.

References: Matthew 24:15 - "Therefore when you see the 'abomination of desolation,' spoken of by Daniel the prophet, standing in the holy place (whoever reads, let him understand)."

The Desolator

1. The Figure of Desolation

Interpretation: The figure who brings desolation is often identified with the Antichrist or a future oppressive ruler who commits sacrilegious acts in the temple, causing desolation.

References: 2 Thessalonians 2:3-4 - "Let no one deceive you by any means; for that Day will not come unless the falling away comes first, and the man of sin is revealed, the son of perdition, who opposes and exalts himself above all that is called God or that is worshiped, so that he sits as God in the temple of God, showing himself that he is God."

The Consummation

1. The End of Desolation

Interpretation: The term "consummation" (H3617 - kalah) refers to the completion or fulfillment of a determined end. This indicates that the period of desolation will come to an end according to God's predetermined plan.

References: Revelation 19:20 - "Then the beast was captured, and with him the false prophet who worked signs in his presence, by which he deceived those who received the mark of the beast and those who worshiped his image. These two were cast alive into the lake of fire burning with brimstone."

Conclusion

The prophecy of the seventy weeks in Daniel 9 is a detailed and profound revelation of God's plan for Israel and the world. The Anointed One (Messiah) and the covenant are central elements of this prophecy, highlighting the arrival and sacrificial death of Jesus Christ, as well as the establishment of a new covenant. The prophecy also points to future events involving the cessation of sacrifices, the rise of an abominable figure, and the ultimate fulfillment of God's redemptive plan.

Understanding these elements within the context of the seventy weeks provides deeper insight into the fulfillment of biblical prophecy and God's sovereignty over history. As we continue to explore the prophetic symbols in the Book of Daniel, the insights gained from the Anointed One and the Covenant will deepen our understanding of the broader prophetic narrative and God's overarching plan for redemption and restoration.

CHAPTER 12

THE HUNT FOR GOLD

The prophecy of the seventy weeks in Daniel 9:24-27 holds profound significance for the Jewish people and the broader scope of Messianic prophecy. This chapter delves into the implications of this prophecy for the Jewish people, exploring how it addresses their historical experiences, covenant relationship with God, and the anticipation of the Messiah. By examining these elements, we aim to provide a comprehensive understanding of the prophecy's significance and its fulfillment in the context of biblical eschatology.

The Seventy Weeks Prophecy

Daniel 9:24-27 - "Seventy sweeks are determined for your people and for your holy city, to finish the transgression, to make an end of sins, to make reconciliation for iniquity, to bring in everlasting righteousness, to seal up vision and prophecy, and to anoint the Most Holy. Know therefore and understand, that from the going forth of the command to restore and build Jerusalem until Messiah the Prince, there shall be seven weeks and sixty-two weeks; the street shall be built again, and the wall, even in troublesome times. And after the sixty-two weeks Messiah shall be cut off, but not for Himself; and the people of the prince who is to come shall destroy the city and the sanctuary. The end of it shall be with a flood, and till the end of the war desolations are determined. Then he shall confirm a covenant with many for one week; but in the middle of the week, he shall bring an end to sacrifice and offering. And on the wing of abominations shall be one who makes desolate, even until the consummation, which is determined, is poured out on the desolate."

Significance for the Jewish People

Historical Context and Exile

1. The Babylonian Exile

Background: The seventy-week prophecy was given during the Babylonian exile, a period of intense suffering and reflection for the Jewish people. The exile was a result of their disobedience and idolatry, leading to the destruction of Jerusalem and the Temple in 586 B.C.

References: 2 Kings 25:8-9 - "In the fifth month, on the seventh day of the month (which was the nineteenth year of King Nebuchadnezzar king of Babylon), Nebuzaradan the captain of the guard, a servant of the king of Babylon, came to Jerusalem. He burned the house of the Lord and the king's house; all the houses of Jerusalem, that is, all the houses of the great, he burned with fire."

2. The Promise of Restoration

Prophetic Promise: Despite their exile, God promised to restore His people and bring them back to their land. The seventy weeks prophecy provided a timeline for this restoration, giving hope and assurance to the exiled community.

References: Jeremiah 29:10-11 - "For thus says the Lord: After seventy years are completed at Babylon, I will visit you and perform My good word toward you, and cause you to return to this place. For I know the thoughts that I think toward you, says the Lord, thoughts of peace and not of evil, to give you a future and a hope."

Covenant Relationship

1. Renewal of the Covenant

Covenantal Themes: The prophecy emphasizes the renewal of God's covenant with Israel. The seventy weeks are designed to accomplish several redemptive purposes, including finishing transgression, making an end of sins, and making reconciliation for iniquity.

References: Daniel 9:24 - "Seventy weeks are determined for your people and for your holy city, to finish the transgression, to make an end of sins, to make reconciliation for iniquity, to bring in everlasting righteousness, to seal up vision and prophecy, and to anoint the Most Holy."

2. Anointing the Most Holy

Significance: The anointing of the Most Holy (likely referring to the anointing of the Messiah or the consecration of the Holy Place) signifies the restoration of proper worship and the establishment of a righteous order, fulfilling God's promises to His people.

References: Isaiah 61:1-2 - "The Spirit of the Lord God is upon Me because the Lord has anointed Me to preach good tidings to the poor; He has sent Me to heal the brokenhearted, to proclaim liberty to the captives, and the opening of the prison to those who are bound; to proclaim the acceptable year of the Lord, and the day of vengeance of our God; to comfort all who mourn."

Messianic Prophecy

The Coming of the Messiah

1. The Timing of the Messiah's Arrival

Prophetic Timeline: The prophecy specifies that from the decree to restore and rebuild Jerusalem until the arrival of the Messiah the Prince, there would be seven weeks and sixty-two weeks (a total of 483 years). This precise timeline points to the first coming of Jesus Christ.

References: Luke 19:41-44 - "Now as He drew near, He saw the city and wept over it, saying, 'If you had known, even you, especially in this your day, the things that make for your peace! But now they are hidden from your eyes. For days will come upon you when your enemies will build an embankment around you, surround you and close you in on every side, and level you, and your children within you, to the ground; and they will not leave in you one stone upon another, because you did not know the time of your visitation.'"

2. The Sacrificial Death of the Messiah

Atonement: The prophecy foretells that the Messiah will be "cut off, but not for Himself," indicating His sacrificial death for the sins of others. This aligns with the concept of the suffering servant in Isaiah 53, who bears the iniquities of humanity.

References: Isaiah 53:5-6 - "But He was wounded for our transgressions, He was bruised for our iniquities; the chastisement for our peace was upon Him, and by His stripes we are healed. All we like sheep have gone astray; we have turned, everyone, to his own way; and the Lord has laid on Him the iniquity of us all."

The Establishment of the New Covenant

1. The Confirmation of the Covenant

New Covenant: The prophecy mentions a covenant being confirmed with many for one week. This is often interpreted as the New Covenant established by Jesus through His death and resurrection, bringing salvation to both Jews and Gentiles.

References: Hebrews 9:15 - "And for this reason He is the Mediator of the new covenant, by means of death, for the redemption of the transgressions under the first covenant, that those who are called may receive the promise of the eternal inheritance."

2. The End of Sacrifice and Offering

Fulfillment: The prophecy indicates that in the middle of the final week, sacrifice and offering would cease. This is seen as the fulfillment of the sacrificial system through the once-for-all sacrifice of Jesus Christ.

References: Hebrews 10:10-12 - "By that will we have been sanctified through the offering of the body of Jesus Christ once for all. And every priest stands ministering daily and offering repeatedly the same sacrifices, which can never take away sins. But this Man, after He had offered one sacrifice for sins forever, sat down at the right hand of God."

The Future Fulfillment and Eschatological Significance

The Final Week and the End Times

1. The Final Seven Years

Eschatology: The final week of the seventy weeks prophecy is often associated with future events, including the end times and the tribulation period. This period involves significant prophetic activities, including the confirmation of a covenant and the cessation of sacrifices.

References: Revelation 13:5-7 - "And he was given a mouth speaking great things and blasphemies, and he was given authority to continue for forty-two months. Then he opened his mouth in blasphemy against God, to blaspheme His name, His tabernacle, and those who dwell in heaven. It was granted to him to make war with the saints and to overcome them. And authority was given him over every tribe, tongue, and nation."

2. The Abomination of Desolation

Future Events: The prophecy also mentions the abomination of desolation, an event associated with the desecration of a holy place. This is linked to the activities of a future oppressive ruler, often identified with the Antichrist.

References: Matthew 24:15 - "Therefore when you see the 'abomination of desolation,' spoken of by Daniel the prophet, standing in the holy place (whoever reads, let him understand)."

Conclusion

The prophecy of the seventy weeks in Daniel 9 is of profound significance for the Jewish people and the broader scope of Messianic prophecy. It addresses their historical experiences, emphasizing their covenant relationship with God and providing a timeline for restoration and redemption. The prophecy's precise predictions regarding the coming and sacrificial death of the Messiah offer compelling evidence of its divine origin and fulfillment.

Furthermore, the prophecy's implications extend into the future, offering insights into end-times events and the ultimate fulfillment of God's redemptive plan. As we continue to explore the prophetic symbols in the Book of Daniel, the significance of the seventy-week prophecy deepens our understanding of God's sovereignty, faithfulness, and the ultimate establishment of His kingdom. This prophecy serves as a powerful reminder of God's control over history and His unwavering commitment to His promises.

CHAPTER 13

A GLITTERING OBSESSION

Daniel Chapter 10 presents a profound vision that has captivated scholars and theologians for centuries. The vision of a glorious man, often interpreted as a Christophany (a pre-incarnate appearance of Christ), offers a vivid and detailed description that conveys immense power, majesty, and divine authority. This chapter will focus on the description of the glorious man as presented in Daniel 10, examining the significance of each element and its implications within the broader context of biblical prophecy.

The Vision of the Glorious Man

Daniel 10:4-9 - "Now on the twenty-fourth day of the first month, as I was by the side of the great river, that is, the Tigris, I lifted my eyes and looked, and behold, a certain man clothed in linen, whose waist was girded with gold of Uphaz! His body was like beryl, his face like the appearance of lightning, his eyes like torches of fire, his arms and feet like burnished bronze in color, and the sound of his words like the voice of a multitude. And I, Daniel, alone saw the vision, for the men who were with me did not see the vision; but a great terror fell upon them, so that they fled to hide. Therefore, I was left alone when I saw this great vision, and no strength remained in me; for my vigor was turned to frailty in me, and I retained no strength. Yet I heard the sound of his words; and while I heard the sound of his words I was in a deep sleep on my face, with my face to the ground."

The Detailed Description of the Glorious Man Clothed in Linen

Daniel 10:5 - "I lifted my eyes and looked, and behold, a certain man clothed in linen..."

1. Symbolism of Linen

Purity and Priesthood: Linen garments are often associated with purity, holiness, and priestly duties in the Bible. The glorious man's clothing signifies his purity and possibly his priestly role.

References: Exodus 28:39 - "You shall skillfully weave the tunic of fine linen thread, you shall make the turban of fine linen, and you shall make the sash of woven work."

Waist Girded with Gold of Uphaz

Daniel 10:5 - "...whose waist was girded with gold of Uphaz!"

1. Symbolism of Gold

Royalty and Divinity: Gold signifies royalty, wealth, and divinity. The gold of Uphaz, known for its high quality, highlights the supreme value and divine nature of the glorious man.

References: Revelation 1:13 - "And in the midst of the seven lampstands One like the Son of Man, clothed with a garment down to the feet and girded about the chest with a golden band."

Body Like Beryl

Daniel 10:6 - "His body was like beryl..."

1. Symbolism of Beryl

Beauty and Splendor: Beryl, a precious gemstone, represents beauty, splendor, and the radiance of the divine presence. The description of the body as beryl conveys a sense of otherworldly glory and majesty.

References: Ezekiel 1:16 - "The appearance of the wheels and their workings was like the color of beryl, and all four had the same likeness. The appearance of their workings was, as it were, a wheel in the middle of a wheel."

Face Like the Appearance of Lightning

Daniel 10:6 - "...his face like the appearance of lightning..."

1. Symbolism of Lightning

Power and Awe: Lightning symbolizes power, awe, and divine revelation. The appearance of lightning in the face of the glorious man indicates his overwhelming power and the awe-inspiring nature of his presence.

References: Matthew 28:3 - "His countenance was like lightning, and his clothing as white as snow."

Eyes Like Torches of Fire

Daniel 10:6 - "...his eyes like torches of fire..."

1. Symbolism of Fire

Judgment and Purity: Fire represents judgment, purification, and penetrating insight. The eyes like torches of fire signify the ability to see through deception, judge righteously, and purify.

References: Revelation 1:14 - "His head and hair were white like wool, as white as snow, and His eyes like a flame of fire."

Arms and Feet Like Burnished Bronze

Daniel 10:6 - "...his arms and feet like burnished bronze in color..."

1. Symbolism of Bronze

Strength and Judgment: Burnished bronze symbolizes strength, stability, and judgment. The arms and feet of the glorious man reflect his powerful and unshakeable nature, capable of executing divine judgment.

References: Revelation 1:15 - "His feet were like fine brass, as if refined in a furnace, and His voice as the sound of many waters."

Voice Like the Sound of a Multitude

Daniel 10:6 - "...and the sound of his words like the voice of a multitude."

1. Symbolism of Multitude

Authority and Majesty: A voice like the sound of a multitude represents overwhelming authority, majesty, and the commanding presence of the divine. The glorious man's voice signifies his supreme authority and the impact of his words.

References: Ezekiel 43:2 - "And behold, the glory of the God of Israel came from the way of the east. His voice was like the sound of many waters; and the earth shone with His glory."

The Impact of the Vision on Daniel

Daniel 10:7-9 - "And I, Daniel, alone saw the vision, for the men who were with me did not see the vision; but a great terror fell upon them, so that they fled to hide themselves. Therefore I was left alone when I saw this great vision, and no strength remained in me; for my vigor was turned to frailty in me, and I retained no strength. Yet I heard the sound of his words; and while I heard the sound of his words I was in a deep sleep on my face, with my face to the ground."

Reactions of Daniel and His Companions

1. Companions' Terror

Fear and Flight: The men with Daniel did not see the vision but were overwhelmed by terror, causing them to flee and hide. This reaction underscores the intense and fearsome nature of the divine presence.

References: Acts 9:7 - "And the men who journeyed with him stood speechless, hearing a voice but seeing no one."

2. Daniel's Response

Physical Weakness: Daniel's reaction to the vision includes a loss of strength, turning his vigor to frailty, and falling into a deep sleep with his face to the ground. This response highlights the overwhelming power and holiness of the vision, rendering him physically incapacitated.

References: Revelation 1:17 - "And when I saw Him, I fell at His feet as dead. But He laid His right hand on me, saying to me, 'Do not be afraid; I am the First and the Last.'"

The Significance of the Glorious Man

Christophany Interpretation

1. Pre-Incarnate Christ

Divine Revelation: Many scholars and theologians interpret the vision of the glorious man as a Christophany, a pre-incarnate appearance of Jesus Christ. The description aligns with other biblical portrayals of Christ in His glorified state, emphasizing His divine nature and authority.

References: John 1:14 - "And the Word became flesh and dwelt among us, and we beheld His glory, the glory as of the only begotten of the Father, full of grace and truth."

Implications for Biblical Prophecy

1. Authority and Sovereignty

Divine Control: The vision reinforces the themes of divine authority and sovereignty over the affairs of humanity. The presence of the glorious man signifies God's direct involvement and control over the unfolding of prophetic events.

References: Colossians 1:16-17 - "For by Him all things were created that are in heaven and that are on earth, visible and invisible, whether thrones or dominions or principalities or powers. All things were created through Him and for Him. And He is before all things, and in Him all things consist."

2. Encouragement and Assurance

Divine Presence: For Daniel and future readers, the vision serves as an encouragement and assurance of God's presence and faithfulness. It reminds believers that God is actively engaged in history and will fulfill His promises.

References: Matthew 28:20 - "...and lo, I am with you always, even to the end of the age. Amen."

Conclusion

The detailed description of the glorious man in Daniel 10 offers a powerful and awe-inspiring glimpse into the divine presence. Each element of the description—from the linen clothing and golden girdle to the eyes like torches of fire and the voice like a multitude—conveys profound symbolism and theological significance. Interpreted by many as a Christophany, this vision underscores the themes of divine authority, holiness, and the assurance of God's sovereign control over history.

As we continue to explore the prophetic visions in the Book of Daniel, the vision of the glorious man stands out as a central and pivotal moment, reinforcing the message of God's faithfulness and the ultimate fulfillment of His redemptive plan. This vision not only impacts Daniel but also provides enduring encouragement and assurance for all believers, reminding us of the powerful presence and authority of the Lord in our lives.

The Spiritual Battle in the Heavenly Realms

Daniel Chapter 10 not only presents a vision of a glorious man but also reveals a profound spiritual battle taking place in the heavenly realms. This chapter focuses on the spiritual warfare that is described in the vision, exploring the implications of these celestial conflicts for the earthly realm. By examining the biblical account and other related scriptures, we aim to provide a comprehensive understanding of the spiritual battle in the heavenly realms.

The Spiritual Battle Revealed

Daniel 10:10-14 - "Suddenly, a hand touched me, which made me tremble on my knees and on the palms of my hands. And he said to me, 'O Daniel, man greatly beloved, understand the words that I speak to you, and stand upright, for I have now been sent to you.' While he was speaking this word to me, I stood trembling. Then he said to me, 'Do not fear, Daniel, for from the first day that you set your heart to understand and to humble yourself before your God, your words were heard; and I have come because of your words. But the prince of the kingdom of Persia withstood me twenty-one days; and behold, Michael, one of the chief princes, came to help me, for I had been left alone there with the kings of Persia. Now I have come to make you understand what will happen to your people in the latter days, for the vision refers to many days yet to come.'"

The Conflict in the Heavenly Realms

The Delayed Response

1. Angelic Messenger

Daniel 10:12-13 - "Then he said to me, 'Do not fear, Daniel, for from the first day that you set your heart to understand and to humble yourself before your God, your words were heard; and I have come because of your words. But the prince of the kingdom of Persia withstood me twenty-one days; and behold, Michael, one of the chief princes, came to help me, for I had been left alone there with the kings of Persia.'"

Significance: An angelic messenger is sent to Daniel in response to his prayers, but the messenger's arrival is delayed by twenty-one days due to resistance from the "prince of the kingdom of Persia," indicating a spiritual conflict in the heavenly realms.

References: Hebrews 1:14 - "Are they not all ministering spirits sent forth to minister for those who will inherit salvation?"

The Prince of Persia

1. Spiritual Opposition

Daniel 10:13 - "But the prince of the kingdom of Persia withstood me twenty-one days..."

Interpretation: The "prince of the kingdom of Persia" is understood to be a powerful demonic entity or spiritual force that exercises influence over the Persian Empire. This indicates the presence of spiritual beings engaged in warfare against God's purposes.

References: Ephesians 6:12 - "For we do not wrestle against flesh and blood, but against principalities, against powers, against the rulers of the darkness of this age, against spiritual hosts of wickedness in the heavenly places."

Michael the Archangel

1. Michael's Assistance

Daniel 10:13 - "...and behold, Michael, one of the chief princes, came to help me..."

Significance: Michael, identified as one of the chief princes or archangels, intervenes to assist the angelic messenger, indicating his role as a protector and warrior in the heavenly realms.

References: Revelation 12:7-9 - "And war broke out in heaven: Michael and his angels fought with the dragon, and the dragon and his angels fought, but they did not prevail, nor was a place found for them in heaven any longer. So the great dragon was cast out, that serpent of old called the Devil and Satan, who deceives the whole world; he was cast to the earth, and his angels were cast out with him."

The Nature of Spiritual Warfare

Cosmic Conflict

1. The Reality of Spiritual Battles

Daniel 10:13 - "But the prince of the kingdom of Persia withstood me twenty-one days..."

Explanation: This passage highlights the reality of ongoing spiritual battles in the heavenly realms. These conflicts involve angelic and demonic forces engaged in warfare over the affairs of nations and the fulfillment of God's plans.

References: Daniel 12:1 - "At that time Michael shall stand up, the great prince who stands watch over the sons of your people; and there shall be a time of trouble, such as never was since there was a nation, even to that time. And at that time your people shall be delivered, everyone who is found written in the book."

The Role of Prayer and Fasting

1. Daniel's Role

Daniel 10:2-3 - "In those days I, Daniel, was mourning three full weeks. I ate no pleasant food, no meat or wine came into my mouth, nor did I anoint myself at all, till three whole weeks were fulfilled."

Significance: Daniel's prayer and fasting played a crucial role in the spiritual battle. His commitment to seeking God and humbling himself facilitated the angelic intervention and the subsequent revelation of the vision.

References: Matthew 17:21 - "However, this kind does not go out except by prayer and fasting."

Implications for Believers

The Importance of Spiritual Vigilance

1. Awareness of Spiritual Warfare

Ephesians 6:10-11 - "Finally, my brethren, be strong in the Lord and in the power of His might. Put on the whole armor of God, that you may be able to stand against the wiles of the devil."

Explanation: Believers are called to be aware of the spiritual battles that occur beyond the physical realm and to remain vigilant and spiritually prepared to engage in this warfare.

References: 1 Peter 5:8 - "Be sober, be vigilant; because your adversary the devil walks about like a roaring lion, seeking whom he may devour."

The Power of Prayer and Fasting

1. Spiritual Discipline

James 5:16 - "Confess your trespasses to one another, and pray for one another, that you may be healed. The effective, fervent prayer of a righteous man avails much."

Explanation: The account of Daniel underscores the power and effectiveness of prayer and fasting in spiritual warfare. These disciplines can influence the heavenly realms and bring about divine intervention and revelation.

References: Isaiah 58:6 - "Is this not the fast that I have chosen: to loose the bonds of wickedness, to undo the heavy burdens, to let the oppressed go free, and that you break every yoke?"

The Assurance of Divine Assistance

1. Angelic Help

Hebrews 1:14 - "Are they not all ministering spirits sent forth to minister for those who will inherit salvation?"

Explanation: Believers can take comfort in knowing that God provides angelic assistance and protection. Angels are actively involved in the spiritual battles that affect our lives and are sent to help and minister to us.

References: Psalm 91:11 - "For He shall give His angels charge over you, to keep you in all your ways."

Conclusion

Daniel Chapter 10 provides a compelling glimpse into the spiritual battle in the heavenly realms, revealing the ongoing conflict between angelic and demonic forces. The delayed response to Daniel's prayer, the intervention of Michael the archangel, and the role of the prince of Persia highlight the reality of cosmic warfare that influences earthly events.

This chapter emphasizes the importance of prayer, fasting, and spiritual vigilance for believers. It reminds us of the power of our spiritual disciplines to affect the heavenly realms and bring about divine intervention. Moreover, it assures us of God's provision of angelic assistance and His sovereign control over all spiritual battles.

As we continue to explore the prophetic visions in the Book of Daniel, the account of the spiritual battle in Chapter 10 enriches our understanding of the broader cosmic conflict and our role within it. This revelation encourages us to remain steadfast in prayer and to trust in God's ultimate victory over all spiritual adversaries.

The Message of Encouragement to Daniel

In Daniel Chapter 10, amidst the profound and intense visions of spiritual warfare and celestial beings, there is a significant message of encouragement given to Daniel. This message is delivered by an angelic messenger and provides assurance, strength, and insight to Daniel. This chapter focuses on the elements of this divine encouragement, exploring its meaning and implications for Daniel and, by extension, for believers today.

The Context of the Encouragement

Daniel 10:10-12 - "Suddenly, a hand touched me, which made me tremble on my knees and on the palms of my hands. And he said to me, 'O Daniel, man greatly beloved, understand the words that I speak to you, and stand upright, for I have now been sent to you.' While he was speaking this word to me, I stood trembling. Then he said to me, 'Do not fear, Daniel, for from the first day that you set your heart to understand and to humble yourself before your God, your words were heard; and I have come because of your words.'"

Elements of the Encouragement

1. The Touch of the Divine Messenger

Daniel 10:10 - "Suddenly, a hand touched me, which made me tremble on my knees and on the palms of my hands."

1. Physical Reassurance

Significance: The touch of the angelic messenger physically reassures Daniel, helping him regain strength and composure. This physical interaction highlights the compassionate nature of divine encounters and the importance of reassurance during overwhelming experiences.

References: Matthew 17:7 - "But Jesus came and touched them and said, 'Arise, and do not be afraid.'"

2. Recognition of Daniel's Beloved Status

Daniel 10:11 - "And he said to me, 'O Daniel, man greatly beloved, understand the words that I speak to you, and stand upright, for I have now been sent to you.'"

1. Assurance of God's Love

Significance: The angelic messenger addresses Daniel as "man greatly beloved," affirming God's deep love and favor towards him. This recognition reassures Daniel of his value and importance in God's eyes, providing comfort and encouragement.

References: John 15:9 - "As the Father loved Me, I also have loved you; abide in My love."

3. Command to Stand Upright

Daniel 10:11 - "...understand the words that I speak to you, and stand upright, for I have now been sent to you."

1. Call to Strength and Readiness

Significance: The command to stand upright signifies a call to strength, readiness, and attentive listening. It encourages Daniel to prepare himself to receive the forthcoming revelation with confidence and clarity.

References: Ephesians 6:13 - "Therefore take up the whole armor of God, that you may be able to withstand in the evil day, and having done all, to stand."

4. Reassurance and Removal of Fear

Daniel 10:12 - "Then he said to me, 'Do not fear, Daniel, for from the first day that you set your heart to understand and to humble yourself before your God, your words were heard, and I have come because of your words.'"

1. Reassurance of God's Response

Significance: The message "Do not fear" is a common divine reassurance. It emphasizes that Daniel's prayers and humility have been recognized by God from the very beginning. This encouragement highlights God's attentiveness and responsiveness to His faithful servants.

References: Isaiah 41:10 - "Fear not, for I am with you; be not dismayed, for I am your God. I will strengthen you, yes, I will help you, I will uphold you with My righteous right hand."

5. Explanation of the Delay

Daniel 10:13-14 - "But the prince of the kingdom of Persia withstood me twenty-one days; and behold, Michael, one of the chief princes, came to help me, for I had been left alone there with the kings of Persia. Now I have come to make you understand what will happen to your people in the latter days, for the vision refers to many days yet to come."

1. Insight into Spiritual Warfare

Significance: The explanation of the delay due to spiritual warfare provides Daniel with insight into the unseen battles that affect earthly events. It reassures him that the delay was not due to neglect but was part of a larger spiritual conflict.

References: Ephesians 6:12 - "For we do not wrestle against flesh and blood, but against principalities, against powers, against the rulers of the darkness of this age, against spiritual hosts of wickedness in the heavenly places."

Further Encouragement and Strengthening

Daniel 10:15-19 - "When he had spoken such words to me, I turned my face toward the ground and became speechless. And suddenly, one having the likeness of the sons of men touched my lips; then I opened my mouth and spoke, saying to him who stood before me, 'My lord, because of the vision my sorrows have overwhelmed me, and I have retained no strength. For how can this servant of my lord talk with you, my lord? As for me, no strength remains in me now, nor is any breath left in me.' Then again, the one having the likeness of a man touched me and strengthened me. And he said, 'O man greatly beloved, fear not! Peace be to you; be strong, yes, be strong!' So when he spoke to me I was strengthened, and said, 'Let my lord speak, for you have strengthened me.'"

1. Touching and Strengthening Daniel

Daniel 10:16-18 - "And suddenly, one having the likeness of the sons of men touched my lips; then I opened my mouth and spoke... Then again, the one having the likeness of a man touched me and strengthened me."

1. Physical and Emotional Strengthening

Significance: The repeated touches by the angelic messenger symbolize continued support and empowerment. These actions not only strengthen Daniel physically but also provide emotional and spiritual fortitude, enabling him to engage with the vision and message.

References: Isaiah 6:6-7 - "Then one of the seraphim flew to me, having in his hand a live coal which he had taken with the tongs from the altar. And he touched my mouth with it, and said: 'Behold, this has touched your lips; your iniquity is taken away, and your sin purged.'"

2. Declaration of Peace and Strength

Daniel 10:19 - "And he said, 'O man greatly beloved, fear not! Peace be to you; be strong, yes, be strong!' So when he spoke to me I was strengthened, and said, 'Let my lord speak, for you have strengthened me.'"

1. Message of Peace

Significance: The declaration of peace ("Peace be to you") provides Daniel with inner calm and reassurance. This peace, coupled with the command to be strong, empowers Daniel to receive and comprehend the divine message fully.

References: John 14:27 - "Peace I leave with you, The peace I give to you; not as the world gives do I give to you. Let not your heart be troubled, neither let it be afraid."

Implications for Believers

1. God's Attention to Prayers

1. Assurance of Being Heard

Significance: Daniel's experience assures believers that God hears their prayers and responds, even when there are delays. This reassurance encourages persistence and faithfulness in prayer.

References: 1 John 5:14 - "Now this is the confidence that we have in Him, that if we ask anything according to His will, He hears us."

2. The Role of Spiritual Strength

1. Encouragement to Stand Firm

Significance: The encouragement given to Daniel to stand firm and be strong applies to all believers. It emphasizes the importance of spiritual strength and resilience in the face of challenges and spiritual battles.

References: Philippians 4:13 - "I can do all things through Christ who strengthens me."

Conclusion

The message of encouragement to Daniel in Chapter 10 is a powerful testament to God's love, attentiveness, and support for His faithful servants. The angelic reassurances, the physical touches, and the words of peace and strength all serve to empower Daniel to receive and comprehend the divine message.

For believers today, this passage offers profound lessons about the importance of prayer, the reality of spiritual warfare, and the assurance of God's support and encouragement. It reminds us that God is deeply involved in our lives, attentive to our prayers, and ready to provide the strength and peace we need to face any challenges.

As we continue to explore the prophetic visions in the Book of Daniel, the message of encouragement in Chapter 10 stands out as a beacon of hope and assurance, reinforcing our faith in God's unwavering commitment to His people and His sovereign control over all events.

CHAPTER 14

NATURE'S WRATH

Daniel Chapter 11 presents a detailed and complex prophecy concerning the conflicts between the kings of the North and South. This chapter explores the historical fulfillment of these prophecies, tracing the intricate and often tumultuous events that align with the visions received by Daniel. By examining the historical context and specific events, we aim to provide a comprehensive understanding of how these prophecies were fulfilled.

The Prophetic Overview

Daniel 11:2-4 - "And now I will tell you the truth: Behold, three more kings will arise in Persia, and the fourth shall be far richer than them all; by his strength, through his riches, he shall stir up all against the realm of Greece. Then a mighty king shall arise, who shall rule with great dominion, and do according to his will. And when he has arisen, his kingdom shall be broken up and divided toward the four winds of heaven, but not among his posterity nor according to his dominion with which he ruled; for his kingdom shall be uprooted, even for others besides these."

The Rise and Division of the Persian Empire

The Kings of Persia

1. The Fourth King: Xerxes I

Daniel 11:2 - "Behold, three more kings will arise in Persia, and the fourth shall be far richer than them all; by his strength, through his riches, he shall stir up all against the realm of Greece."

Historical Context: The three kings after Cyrus the Great were Cambyses, Smerdis (Pseudo-Smerdis), and Darius I. The fourth king, Xerxes I, was indeed far richer and led the Persian Empire in a major campaign against Greece, which culminated in the famous battles of Thermopylae and Salamis.

References: Xerxes' wealth and military campaigns are well-documented in historical records, particularly in the works of Herodotus and other ancient historians.

The Rise of Greece

1. Alexander the Great

Daniel 11:3 - "Then a mighty king shall arise, who shall rule with great dominion, and do according to his will."

Historical Context: Alexander the Great fits this description perfectly. He rose swiftly to power and established a vast empire that stretched from Greece to Egypt and into northwest India.

References: Alexander's conquests are among the most famous in history, marked by decisive battles such as Issus and Gaugamela.

The Division of Alexander's Empire

1. The Diadochi

Daniel 11:4 - "And when he has arisen, his kingdom shall be broken up and divided toward the four winds of heaven, but not among his posterity nor according to his dominion with which he ruled; for his kingdom shall be uprooted, even for others besides these."

Historical Context: After Alexander's death in 323 B.C., his empire was divided among his generals, known as the Diadochi. The four main divisions were the Ptolemaic Kingdom in Egypt, the Seleucid Empire in Syria and Persia, the Kingdom of Lysimachus in Thrace and Asia Minor, and the Antigonid dynasty in Macedonia and Greece.

References: This division is well-documented and had significant implications for the subsequent history of the Hellenistic world.

The Kings of the North and South

The Ptolemaic and Seleucid Dynasties

1. The King of the South: Ptolemy I Soter

Daniel 11:5 - "Also the king of the South shall become strong, as well as one of his princes; and he shall gain power over him and have dominion. His dominion shall be a great dominion."

Historical Context: Ptolemy I Soter, a former general under Alexander, established the Ptolemaic Kingdom in Egypt, which became a major Hellenistic power.

References: The Ptolemaic Kingdom is noted for its cultural and economic prosperity, with Alexandria as a major center of learning and commerce.

2. The King of the North: Seleucus I Nicator

Daniel 11:6 - "And at the end of some years they shall join forces, for the daughter of the king of the South shall go to the king of the North to make an agreement; but she shall not retain the power of her authority, and neither he nor his authority shall stand; but she shall be given up, with those who brought her, and with him who begot her and with him who strengthened her in those times."

Historical Context: Seleucus I Nicator established the Seleucid Empire, which controlled a vast region including Syria, Mesopotamia, and Persia. The marriage alliance between Antiochus II Theos (a later Seleucid king) and Berenice, the daughter of Ptolemy II Philadelphus, aimed to secure peace but ultimately failed, leading to further conflicts.

References: The political marriages and subsequent betrayals are well-recorded in historical sources, highlighting the instability and intrigue of the period.

Continued Conflicts and Shifting Alliances

Antiochus III the Great and Ptolemy IV Philopator

1. The Battle of Raphia

Daniel 11:11-12 - "And the king of the South shall be moved with rage, and go out and fight with him, with the king of the North, who shall muster a great multitude; but the multitude shall be given into the hand of his enemy. When he has taken away the multitude, his heart will be lifted up; and he will cast down tens of thousands, but he will not prevail."

Historical Context: The Battle of Raphia in 217 B.C. was a decisive confrontation between Ptolemy IV Philopator of Egypt and Antiochus III the Great of the Seleucid Empire. Ptolemy IV secured a significant victory, but his subsequent actions led to further instability.

References: This battle is a key event in Hellenistic history, marking the ebb and flow of power between the Ptolemaic and Seleucid kingdoms.

Antiochus IV Epiphanes and the Maccabean Revolt

1. The Abomination of Desolation

Daniel 11:31 - "And forces shall be mustered by him, and they shall defile the sanctuary fortress; then they shall take away the daily sacrifices, and place there the abomination of desolation."

Historical Context: Antiochus IV Epiphanes, a Seleucid king, intensified the conflict with the Jewish population by desecrating the Second Temple in Jerusalem, erecting an altar to Zeus, and outlawing Jewish religious practices. This provocation led to the Maccabean Revolt.

References: The actions of Antiochus IV and the subsequent Maccabean Revolt are well-documented in the books of Maccabees and other historical sources, illustrating the intense religious and cultural conflicts of the era.

The Final Conflicts and the Roman Intervention

The Rise of Rome

1. Pompey the Great

Daniel 11:40-45 - "At the time of the end the king of the South shall attack him; and the king of the North shall come against him like a whirlwind, with chariots, horsemen, and with many ships; and he shall enter the countries, overwhelm them, and pass through. He shall also enter the Glorious Land, and many countries shall be overthrown; but these shall escape from his hand: Edom, Moab, and the prominent people of Ammon. He shall stretch out his hand against the countries, and the land of Egypt shall not escape. He shall have power over the treasures of gold and silver, and over all the precious things of Egypt; also the Libyans and Ethiopians shall follow at his heels. But news from the east and the north shall trouble him; therefore he shall go out with great fury to destroy and annihilate many. And he shall plant the tents of his palace between the seas and the glorious holy mountain; yet he shall come to his end, and no one will help him."

Historical Context: The final verses of Daniel 11 are often interpreted as referring to the intervention of Rome in the Hellenistic conflicts. Pompey the Great's conquest of Jerusalem in 63 B.C. and the subsequent incorporation of the Eastern Mediterranean into the Roman Republic mark the end of the Seleucid and Ptolemaic power struggles.

References: Roman intervention fundamentally altered the political landscape of the region, establishing a new era of Roman dominance.

Conclusion

The detailed prophecies in Daniel 11 find remarkable fulfillment in the historical events of the Hellenistic period. From the rise and fall of the Persian Empire, through the conquests and division of Alexander the Great's empire, to the ongoing conflicts between the Ptolemaic and Seleucid dynasties, and finally the rise of Rome, these prophecies demonstrate the precision and accuracy of biblical revelation.

By examining these historical fulfillments, we gain a deeper understanding of the divine orchestration of world events and the interplay of power and politics in ancient history. The prophecy of the kings of the North and South serves as a testament to the reliability of Scripture and God's sovereign control over the affairs of nations.

The Rise of Antiochus IV Epiphanes

Daniel Chapter 11 provides a vivid and detailed prophecy concerning the rise of a figure known as Antiochus IV Epiphanes, one of the most notorious rulers of the Hellenistic period. His reign marked a significant period of conflict, persecution, and cultural upheaval for the Jewish people. This chapter will explore the historical context, political maneuvers, and impact of Antiochus IV's rise to power, examining how his actions fulfilled the prophetic visions outlined in Daniel.

Historical Background

The Seleucid Empire

1. The Foundation of the Seleucid Dynasty

Historical Context: The Seleucid Empire was established following the division of Alexander the Great's empire. Seleucus I Nicator, one of Alexander's generals, founded the empire, which stretched from the Mediterranean Sea to the borders of India. This vast territory included regions that are now part of modern-day Turkey, Syria, Iraq, Iran, and Afghanistan.

References: The historical accounts of the Seleucid Empire are well-documented by ancient historians such as Appian and Polybius.

2. Internal Strife and External Pressures

Political Instability: The Seleucid Empire faced constant internal strife and external pressures, including conflicts with the Ptolemaic Kingdom of Egypt and the rise of the Parthian Empire. These challenges weakened the empire and set the stage for ambitious rulers like Antiochus IV Epiphanes to seize power through intrigue and force.

References: Polybius, Histories, Book 5, provides detailed accounts of the political machinations and military campaigns of the Seleucid rulers.

The Rise of Antiochus IV Epiphanes

Ascension to Power

1. Early Life and Exile

Background: Antiochus IV, originally named Mithridates, was the son of Antiochus III the Great. He spent part of his early life in Rome as a political hostage, which influenced his perspectives and strategies upon returning to the Seleucid court.

References: Livy, History of Rome, Book 35, mentions Antiochus IV's time in Rome and his interactions with Roman society and politics.

2. Seizing the Throne

Daniel 11:21 - "And in his place shall arise a vile person, to whom they will not give the honor of royalty; but he shall come in peaceably, and seize the kingdom by intrigue."

Historical Fulfillment: Antiochus IV came to power through deceit and manipulation. After the death of his brother, Seleucus IV Philopator, Antiochus IV claimed the throne, initially acting as regent for his nephew, the rightful heir, but eventually usurping the throne outright.

References: The account of Antiochus IV's rise to power through intrigue and assassination is detailed in ancient sources such as 1 Maccabees and the writings of Josephus.

The Reign of Antiochus IV Epiphanes

1. Self-Proclaimed Divine Status

Daniel 11:36 - "Then the king shall do according to his own will: he shall exalt and magnify himself above every god, shall speak blasphemies against the God of gods, and shall prosper till the wrath has been accomplished; for what has been determined shall be done."

Self-Deification: Antiochus IV adopted the title "Epiphanes," meaning "God Manifest." He promoted the worship of Greek gods and attempted to impose Hellenistic culture and religion upon his subjects, including the Jewish population.

References: Coins from Antiochus IV's reign bear the inscription "Theos Epiphanes," reflecting his claim to divinity.

2. Persecution of the Jews

Daniel 11:31 - "And forces shall be mustered by him, and they shall defile the sanctuary fortress; then they shall take away the daily sacrifices, and place there the abomination of desolation."

Religious Persecution: Antiochus IV's policies included the desecration of the Second Temple in Jerusalem. He erected an altar to Zeus within the temple precincts and banned Jewish religious practices, leading to widespread persecution.

References: 1 Maccabees 1:41-64 and 2 Maccabees 6:1-11 detail the severe persecution and the specific acts of sacrilege committed by Antiochus IV.

The Abomination of Desolation

Desecration of the Temple

1. The Abomination

Daniel 11:31 - "...and place there the abomination of desolation."

Historical Context: The "abomination of desolation" refers to the pagan altar and idol set up in the Jewish temple, a direct affront to Jewish religious beliefs and practices. This act of sacrilege sparked significant resistance among the Jewish people.

References: The abomination of desolation is also mentioned in the New Testament, reflecting its profound impact on Jewish history and eschatological expectations (Matthew 24:15).

The Maccabean Revolt

1. Jewish Resistance

Daniel 11:32-33 - "Those who do wickedly against the covenant he shall corrupt with flattery; but the people who know their God shall be strong, and carry out great exploits. And those of the people who understand shall instruct many;

yet for many days they shall fall by sword and flame, by captivity and plundering."

Historical Fulfillment: The oppressive policies of Antiochus IV led to the Maccabean Revolt, a significant uprising led by Judas Maccabeus and his brothers. This revolt successfully restored Jewish religious practices and rededicated the temple.

References: The heroic deeds of the Maccabees and the subsequent rededication of the temple are celebrated in the Jewish festival of Hanukkah, as recorded in 1 Maccabees and 2 Maccabees.

The Impact of Antiochus IV's Reign

Short-Term Consequences

1. Temporary Control

Daniel 11:36 - "Then the king shall do according to his own will... and shall prosper till the wrath has been accomplished; for what has been determined shall be done."

Temporary Success: Antiochus IV achieved temporary success in his campaigns and policies, exerting considerable influence over the region and promoting Hellenistic culture aggressively.

References: The expansionist policies and military campaigns of Antiochus IV are detailed in various historical records, illustrating his ambition and temporary successes.

Long-Term Legacy

1. Strengthening Jewish Identity

Result of Persecution: The persecution under Antiochus IV had the unintended consequence of strengthening Jewish identity and religious fervor. The Maccabean Revolt and the subsequent rededication of the temple reinforced the Jewish commitment to their faith and traditions.

References: The books of Maccabees and historical accounts by Josephus emphasize the resilience and renewed dedication of the Jewish people in the face of persecution.

2. Prophetic Fulfillment

Validation of Prophecy: The rise and actions of Antiochus IV Epiphanes serve as a significant fulfillment of the detailed prophecies in Daniel 11. These events validate the prophetic accuracy of the Scriptures and highlight the ongoing spiritual and historical battles faced by God's people.

References: The fulfillment of these prophecies is often cited in theological discussions as evidence of the reliability and divine inspiration of the biblical text.

Conclusion

The rise of Antiochus IV Epiphanes is a pivotal chapter in the history of the Jewish people and the broader Hellenistic world. His reign, marked by ambition, sacrilege, and persecution, fulfilled the detailed prophecies outlined in Daniel 11. The actions of Antiochus IV, including the abomination of desolation and the resulting Maccabean Revolt, had profound short-term and long-term impacts on Jewish identity and religious practices.

By examining the historical fulfillment of these prophecies, we gain a deeper understanding of the intricate interplay between divine sovereignty and human history. The reign of Antiochus IV serves as a testament to the resilience of faith in the face of oppression and the ultimate triumph of God's purposes in history.

The Prophetic Foreshadowing of the Antichrist

Daniel Chapter 11 provides a vivid and detailed prophecy that not only describes historical events but also serves as a prophetic foreshadowing of the Antichrist. Antiochus IV Epiphanes, a significant figure in the Hellenistic period, embodies characteristics and actions that prefigure the ultimate embodiment of evil in eschatological prophecy: the Antichrist. This chapter will explore the connections between Antiochus IV and the Antichrist, examining the prophetic foreshadowing presented in the Book of Daniel and other biblical texts.

Characteristics of Antiochus IV Epiphanes

Ambition and Deception

Daniel 11:21 - "And in his place shall arise a vile person, to whom they will not give the honor of royalty; but he shall come in peaceably, and seize the kingdom by intrigue."

1. Deceptive Rise to Power

Historical Context: Antiochus IV Epiphanes seized power through deceit and political maneuvering, rather than through legitimate succession. His rise to power was marked by intrigue and manipulation.

References: 1 Maccabees 1:10 - "And there came out of them a wicked root, Antiochus Epiphanes, son of Antiochus the king, who had been a hostage at Rome, and he reigned in the hundred and thirty-seventh year of the kingdom of the Greeks."

Blasphemy and Self-Exaltation

Daniel 11:36 - "Then the king shall do according to his own will: he shall exalt and magnify himself above every god, shall speak blasphemies against the God of gods, and shall prosper till the wrath has been accomplished; for what has been determined shall be done."

1. Claim to Divinity

Self-Deification: Antiochus IV declared himself to be divine, adopting the title "Epiphanes," meaning "God

Manifest." His blasphemous actions and self-exaltation were direct affronts to the Jewish faith and worship of Yahweh.

References: The coins minted during his reign bear the inscription "Theos Epiphanes," showcasing his claim to divinity.

Persecution of the Faithful

Daniel 11:31-32 - "And forces shall be mustered by him, and they shall defile the sanctuary fortress; then they shall take away the daily sacrifices, and place there the abomination of desolation. Those who do wickedly against the covenant he shall corrupt with flattery; but the people who know their God shall be strong, and carry out great exploits."

1. Religious Persecution

Abomination of Desolation: Antiochus IV's desecration of the Second Temple and his prohibition of Jewish religious practices led to severe persecution. His actions forced Jews to choose between compliance with Hellenistic practices and faithfulness to their religious traditions.

References: 1 Maccabees 1:41-43 - "Moreover King Antiochus wrote to his whole kingdom, that all should be one people, and everyone should leave his laws: so all the heathen agreed according to the commandment of the king. Yea, many also of the Israelites consented to his religion, and sacrificed unto idols, and profaned the sabbath."

Foreshadowing the Antichrist

Deceptive Rise to Power

2 Thessalonians 2:9-10 - "The coming of the lawless one is according to the working of Satan, with all power, signs, and lying wonders, and with all unrighteous deception among those who perish, because they did not receive the love of the truth, that they might be saved."

1. Deception and Intrigue

Comparison: The Antichrist, like Antiochus IV, will rise to power through deception and intrigue. His ascent will be marked by false promises and manipulative tactics, drawing people away from the truth.

References: Revelation 13:14 - "And he deceives those who dwell on the earth by those signs which he was granted to do in the sight of the beast, telling those who dwell on the earth to make an image to the beast who was wounded by the sword and lived."

Self-Exaltation and Blasphemy

2 Thessalonians 2:4 - "Who opposes and exalts himself above all that is called God or that is worshiped, so that he sits as God in the temple of God, showing himself that he is God."

1. Claim to Divinity and Blasphemy

Comparison: The Antichrist will exalt himself above all gods and demand worship, much like Antiochus IV. His blasphemous claims and actions will be direct affronts to the true God, seeking to establish his own divine status.

References: Revelation 13:5-6 - "And he was given a mouth speaking great things and blasphemies, and he was given authority to continue for forty-two months. Then he opened his mouth in blasphemy against God, to blaspheme His name, His tabernacle, and those who dwell in heaven."

Persecution of the Faithful

Revelation 13:7 - "It was granted to him to make war with the saints and to overcome them. And authority was given him over every tribe, tongue, and nation."

1. Persecution and Martyrdom

Comparison: The Antichrist will engage in severe persecution of believers, similar to the actions of Antiochus IV. He will wage war against the saints, seeking to eradicate true worship and impose his authority.

References: Daniel 7:25 - "He shall speak pompous words against the Most High, shall persecute the saints of the Most High, and shall intend to change times and law. Then the saints shall be given into his hand for a time and times and half a time."

The Abomination of Desolation

Historical and Future Fulfillment

Matthew 24:15-16 - "Therefore when you see the 'abomination of desolation,' spoken of by Daniel the prophet, standing in the holy place (whoever reads, let him understand), then let those who are in Judea flee to the mountains."

1. Antiochus IV's Actions

Historical Context: Antiochus IV's desecration of the Temple in Jerusalem serves as a historical precedent for the ultimate abomination of desolation that will be committed by the Antichrist.

References: 1 Maccabees 1:54 - "Now the fifteenth day of the month Casleu, in the hundred forty and fifth year, they set up the abomination of desolation upon the altar, and builded idol altars throughout the cities of Judah on every side."

2. Future Fulfillment

Eschatological Significance: Jesus referenced the abomination of desolation in the Olivet Discourse, indicating that a future event similar to the actions of Antiochus IV will occur under the Antichrist's reign. This event will signal the intensification of the Great Tribulation.

References: 2 Thessalonians 2:3-4 - "Let no one deceive you by any means; for that Day will not come unless the falling away comes first, and the man of sin is revealed, the son of perdition, who opposes and exalts himself above all that is called God or that is worshiped, so that he sits as God in the temple of God, showing himself that he is God."

The Ultimate Defeat

Divine Judgment

Daniel 11:45 - "And he shall plant the tents of his palace between the seas and the glorious holy mountain; yet he shall come to his end, and no one will help him."

1. Antiochus IV's Demise

Historical Context: Despite his power and blasphemous actions, Antiochus IV met his end without assistance, illustrating the ultimate futility of his rebellion against God.

References: 2 Maccabees 9:28 - "Thus the murderer and blasphemer having suffered most grievously, as he entreated other men to be delivered from death, it came to pass that in this manner he died a miserable death in a strange country in the mountains."

The Antichrist's Defeat

Revelation 19:20 - "Then the beast was captured, and with him the false prophet who worked signs in his presence, by which he deceived those who received the mark of the beast and those who worshiped his image. These two were cast alive into the lake of fire burning with brimstone."

1. Eschatological Fulfillment

Divine Judgment: The Antichrist, like Antiochus IV, will face divine judgment and ultimate defeat. His reign of terror will be brought to an end by the return of Christ, who will establish His righteous kingdom.

References: Daniel 7:26-27 - "But the court shall be seated, and they shall take away his dominion, to consume and destroy it forever. Then the kingdom and dominion, and the greatness of the kingdoms under the whole heaven, shall be given to the people, the saints of the Most High. His kingdom is an everlasting kingdom, and all dominions shall serve and obey Him."

Conclusion

The rise and actions of Antiochus IV Epiphanes serve as a prophetic foreshadowing of the Antichrist. Through his deceptive rise to power, self-exaltation, blasphemy, and persecution of the faithful, Antiochus IV provides a historical template for understanding the future actions and characteristics of the Antichrist.

The abomination of desolation committed by Antiochus IV prefigures the ultimate sacrilege that will be carried out by the Antichrist, signaling the intensification of the Great Tribulation.

By examining these prophetic parallels, we gain a deeper understanding of the eschatological significance of these events and the ultimate triumph of God's kingdom over the forces of evil. The detailed prophecies in Daniel and their historical and future fulfillments underscore the reliability of Scripture and the certainty of God's sovereign plan. As believers, we are encouraged to remain vigilant, faithful, and hopeful, knowing that despite the rise of evil, God's ultimate victory is assured.

CHAPTER 15

SHIFTING FORTUNES

Daniel Chapter 12, the final chapter of the Book of Daniel, shifts the focus to eschatological events—the time of the end. This chapter examines the profound themes of resurrection and judgment, providing a glimpse into the culmination of history and the fulfillment of God's redemptive plan. By exploring the detailed prophecy in Daniel 12 and related biblical texts, we aim to understand the significance of the resurrection and judgment within the broader context of biblical eschatology.

The Prophetic Context

Daniel 12:1-3 - "At that time Michael shall stand up, the great prince who stands watch over the sons of your people; and there shall be a time of trouble, such as never was since there was a nation, even to that time. And at that time your people shall be delivered, everyone who is found written in the book. And many of those who sleep in the dust of the earth shall awake, some to everlasting life, some to shame and everlasting contempt. Those who are wise shall shine like the brightness of the firmament, and those who turn many to righteousness like the stars forever and ever."

The Time of Trouble

The Great Tribulation

1. Unprecedented Distress

Daniel 12:1 - "At that time Michael shall stand up, the great prince who stands watch over the sons of your people; and there shall be a time of trouble, such as never was since there was a nation, even to that time."

Explanation: This period of unprecedented distress, often referred to as the Great Tribulation, signifies a time of intense suffering and turmoil preceding the end times. Michael the archangel, a protector of Israel, stands up to defend God's people during this crucial period.

References: Matthew 24:21 - "For then there will be great tribulation, such as has not been since the beginning of the world until this time, no, nor ever shall be."

The Deliverance of God's People

The Book of Life

1. Divine Deliverance

Daniel 12:1 - "And at that time your people shall be delivered, everyone who is found written in the book."

Explanation: The deliverance mentioned refers to the salvation and protection of those whose names are written in the Book of life. This divine record signifies those who belong to God and are destined for eternal life.

References: Revelation 20:12 - "And I saw the dead, small and great, standing before God, and books were opened. And another book was opened, which is the Book of Life. And the dead were judged according to their works, by the things which were written in the books."

The Resurrection

The Awakening from Death

Daniel 12:2 - "And many of those who sleep in the dust of the earth shall awake, some to everlasting life, some to shame and everlasting contempt."

1. The Resurrection of the Dead

Explanation: This verse clearly describes the resurrection of the dead, a cornerstone of Christian eschatological hope. The resurrection will involve a physical reawakening of those who have died, leading to either eternal life or eternal judgment.

References: John 5:28-29 - "Do not marvel at this; for the hour is coming in which all who are in the graves will hear

His voice and come forth—those who have done good, to the resurrection of life, and those who have done evil, to the resurrection of condemnation."

The Judgment

Eternal Destinies

1. Everlasting Life and Everlasting Contempt

Daniel 12:2 - "...some to everlasting life, some to shame and everlasting contempt."

Explanation: The resurrection leads to a final judgment where individuals are assigned their eternal destinies. Those who are righteous and faithful will receive everlasting life, while those who are wicked and rebellious will face shame and everlasting contempt.

References: Matthew 25:46 - "And these will go away into everlasting punishment, but the righteous into eternal life."

The Reward of the Righteous

Shining Like the Stars

Daniel 12:3 - "Those who are wise shall shine like the brightness of the firmament, and those who turn many to righteousness like the stars forever and ever."

1. The Glory of the Wise and Righteous

Explanation: This verse highlights the reward for the wise and those who lead others to righteousness. Their glory will be like the brightness of the heavens, reflecting the eternal honor and splendor bestowed upon them by God.

References: Matthew 13:43 - "Then the righteous will shine forth as the sun in the kingdom of their Father. He who has ears to hear, let him hear!"

The Final Judgment

The Great White Throne Judgment

Revelation 20:11-15 - "Then I saw a great white throne and Him who sat on it, from whose face the earth and the heaven fled away. And there was found no place for them. And I saw the dead, small and great, standing before God, and books were opened. And another book was opened, which is the Book of Life. And the dead were judged according to their works, by the things which were written in the books. The sea gave up the dead who were in it, and Death and Hades delivered up the dead who were in them. And they were judged, each one according to his works. Then Death and Hades were cast into the lake of fire. This is the second death. And anyone not found written in the Book of Life was cast into the lake of fire."

1. The Process of Judgment

Explanation: This passage from Revelation provides a detailed description of the final judgment. All the dead will be resurrected and stand before the great white throne of God.

They will be judged according to their works, as recorded in the books, and their eternal destiny will be determined.

References: Hebrews 9:27 - "And as it is appointed for men to die once, but after this the judgment."

The Assurance of Eternal Life

The Promise of Resurrection

John 11:25-26 - "Jesus said to her, 'I am the resurrection and the life. He who believes in Me, though he may die, he shall live. And whoever lives and believes in Me shall never die. Do you believe this?'"

1. Jesus as the Source of Life

Explanation: Jesus' declaration emphasizes that He is the source of resurrection and eternal life. Belief in Him assures believers of eternal life beyond physical death, reinforcing the hope and promise of resurrection.

References: 1 Corinthians 15:52-53 - "In a moment, in the twinkling of an eye, at the last trumpet. For the trumpet will sound, and the dead will be raised incorruptible, and we shall be changed. For this corruptible must put on incorruption, and this mortal must put on immortality."

Conclusion

The themes of resurrection and judgment in Daniel Chapter 12 provide a profound conclusion to the Book of Daniel, emphasizing the ultimate hope and justice that God will bring to His people. The resurrection of the dead and the final judgment are central tenets of Christian eschatology, affirming the belief in eternal life for the righteous and eternal condemnation for the wicked.

Through these prophecies, believers are assured of God's sovereign plan and the ultimate fulfillment of His promises. The promise of resurrection and the certainty of judgment call for a life of faithfulness, righteousness, and hope, as we look forward to the time when God will make all things new and establish His eternal kingdom.

The Sealing of the Book (Daniel 12)

Daniel Chapter 12 concludes the remarkable visions and prophecies given to Daniel with a command to seal the book. This sealing signifies the preservation and confidentiality of the revelations until the appointed time. This chapter will explore the significance of the sealing of the book, its implications for understanding prophecy, and its place within the broader biblical narrative.

The Command to Seal the Book

Daniel 12:4 - "But you, Daniel, shut up the words, and seal the book until the time of the end; many shall run to and fro, and knowledge shall increase."

The Act of Sealing

1. Preservation and Protection

Significance: The command to "shut up the words, and seal the book" indicates the importance of preserving and protecting the revelations given to Daniel. In ancient times, sealing a document was a way to authenticate and safeguard its contents.

References: Isaiah 8:16 - "Bind up the testimony, seal the law among my disciples."

2. Confidentiality and Timing

Significance: Sealing the book implies that its full understanding is reserved for a future time when the knowledge and insight necessary to comprehend it will be available. This timing element suggests that the prophecies contain truths meant for future generations.

References: Revelation 10:4 - "Now when the seven thunders uttered their voices, I was about to write; but I heard a voice from heaven saying to me, 'Seal up the things which the seven thunders uttered, and do not write them.'"

The Time of the End

Increased Knowledge and Understanding

Daniel 12:4 - "...many shall run to and fro, and knowledge shall increase."

1. The Pursuit of Understanding

Interpretation: The phrase "many shall run to and fro" can be understood as a search for understanding and knowledge. This suggests that in the time of the end, people will seek to understand the sealed prophecies with increased fervor.

References: Amos 8:12 - "They shall wander from sea to sea, and from north to east; they shall run to and fro, seeking the word of the Lord, but shall not find it."

2. The Increase of Knowledge

Significance: The increase of knowledge indicates that as the end times approach, there will be greater insight into the prophecies. Advances in understanding, both spiritual and intellectual, will enable a clearer interpretation of the sealed revelations.

References: 1 Corinthians 13:9-10 - "For we know in part and we prophesy in part. But when that which is perfect has come, then that which is in part will be done away."

The Unsealing and Fulfillment

The Appointed Time

Daniel 12:9 - "And he said, 'Go your way, Daniel, for the words are closed up and sealed till the time of the end.'"

1. The Appointed Time of Revelation

Interpretation: The words "closed up and sealed till the time of the end" emphasize that the full understanding of Daniel's prophecies is reserved for a specific future period.

This appointed time will be marked by events and circumstances that will make the meanings clear.

References: Habakkuk 2:3 - "For the vision is yet for an appointed time; but at the end it will speak, and it will not lie. Though it tarries, wait for it; because it will surely come, it will not tarry."

The Role of the Faithful

Daniel 12:10 - "Many shall be purified, made white, and refined, but the wicked shall do wickedly; and none of the wicked shall understand, but the wise shall understand."

1. Purification and Refinement

Significance: Those who are faithful will undergo purification and refinement, making them capable of understanding the prophecies. Their spiritual preparedness will enable them to comprehend the sealed words when the time comes.

References: Malachi 3:3 - "He will sit as a refiner and a purifier of silver; He will purify the sons of Levi, and purge them as gold and silver, that they may offer to the Lord an offering in righteousness."

2. The Wise and the Wicked

Interpretation: A clear distinction is made between the wise, who will understand the prophecies, and the wicked, who will remain in ignorance. This highlights the moral and spiritual dimensions of comprehending divine revelations.

References: Proverbs 28:5 - "Evil men do not understand justice, but those who seek the Lord understand all."

The Opening of the Seals

The Revelation of Jesus Christ

Revelation 5:1-5 - "And I saw in the right hand of Him who sat on the throne a scroll written inside and on the back, sealed with seven seals. Then I saw a strong angel proclaiming with a loud voice, 'Who is worthy to open the scroll and to loose its seals?' And no one in heaven or on the earth or under the earth was able to open the scroll, or to look at it. So I wept much, because no one was found worthy to open and read the scroll, or to look at it. But one of the elders said to me, 'Do not weep. Behold, the Lion of the tribe of Judah, the Root of David, has prevailed to open the scroll and to loose its seven seals.'"

1. The Worthy One

Significance: In the Book of Revelation, the opening of the sealed scroll is accomplished by Jesus Christ, the Lamb of God. This act signifies the unveiling of divine mysteries and the fulfillment of God's plan.

References: Revelation 6:1 - "Now I saw when the Lamb opened one of the seals, and I heard one of the four living creatures saying with a voice like thunder, 'Come and see.'"

The Unveiling of Prophetic Truths

1. The Progressive Revelation

Interpretation: The opening of the seals in Revelation represents the progressive unfolding of God's plan for the end times. Each seal reveals a new aspect of the divine judgment and redemption, leading to the ultimate fulfillment of prophecy.

References: Revelation 10:7 - "But in the days of the sounding of the seventh angel, when he is about to sound, the mystery of God would be finished, as He declared to His servants the prophets."

The Implications for Believers

Preparation and Vigilance

1. Spiritual Readiness

Application: Believers are called to remain vigilant and spiritually prepared for the time when the sealed prophecies will be fully understood. This involves a commitment to purity, wisdom, and faithfulness.

References: Matthew 24:42-44 - "Watch therefore, for you do not know what hour your Lord is coming. But know this, that if the master of the house had known what hour the thief would come, he would have watched and not allowed his house to be broken into. Therefore you also be ready, for the Son of Man is coming at an hour you do not expect."

The Hope of Fulfillment

1. Assurance of God's Sovereignty

Encouragement: The sealing and eventual unsealing of the book remind believers of God's sovereignty and the certainty of His plan. This assurance provides hope and confidence in the face of uncertainty and trials.

References: Romans 8:28 - "And we know that all things work together for good to those who love God, to those who are the called according to His purpose."

Conclusion

The command to seal the book in Daniel Chapter 12 underscores the importance of preserving divine revelations for their appointed time. This act of sealing signifies both protection and confidentiality, ensuring that the prophecies will be understood when the necessary knowledge and insight are available. The process of unsealing, as depicted in the Book of Revelation, highlights the progressive unfolding of God's plan through Jesus Christ.

For believers, the sealing of the book emphasizes the need for spiritual readiness, wisdom, and faithfulness. It assures us of God's sovereignty and the ultimate fulfillment of His prophetic promises. As we await the time of the end, we are encouraged to live in vigilance and hope, trusting in the divine plan that will be revealed in its fullness at the appointed time.

The Time, Times, and Half a Time

Daniel Chapter 12 mentions the enigmatic phrase "time, times, and half a time," which has intrigued and puzzled scholars and theologians for centuries. This phrase appears in the context of prophetic visions and symbolizes a specific period within the eschatological timeline. This chapter will explore the meaning and implications of "time, times, and half a time," examining its occurrence in the Book of Daniel and other biblical texts to gain a comprehensive understanding of its significance.

The Prophetic Phrase

Daniel 12:7 - "Then I heard the man clothed in linen, who was above the waters of the river, when he held up his right hand and his left hand to heaven, and swore by Him who lives forever, that it shall be for a time, times, and half a time; and when the power of the holy people has been completely shattered, all these things shall be finished."

Understanding the Phrase

The Components

1. Time

Interpretation: The term "time" typically represents one unit of measurement, often understood as one year in prophetic literature.

References: Daniel 4:16 - "Let his heart be changed from that of a man, let him be given the heart of a beast, and let seven times pass over him."

2. Times

Interpretation: "Times" is understood as a doubling of the unit, representing two years.

3. Half a Time

Interpretation: "Half a time" represents half of the initial unit, equating to six months.

Combined Duration: Therefore, "time, times, and half a time" totals to three and a half years.

Occurrences in Daniel and Revelation

Daniel's Visions

1. The Little Horn

Daniel 7:25 - "He shall speak pompous words against the Most High, shall persecute the saints of the Most High, and shall intend to change times and law. Then the saints shall be given into his hand for a time and times and half a time."

Interpretation: In this vision, the "little horn" (interpreted as a representation of an oppressive ruler or the

Antichrist) will dominate and persecute the saints for a period of three and a half years.

References: This period is also associated with significant tribulation and upheaval, reflecting a time of intense persecution and suffering for the faithful.

Revelation's Confirmation

1. The Woman and the Dragon

Revelation 12:14 - "But the woman was given two wings of a great eagle, that she might fly into the wilderness to her place, where she is nourished for a time and times and half a time, from the presence of the serpent."

Interpretation: The woman, symbolizing God's people, is protected and sustained in the wilderness for three and a half years, away from the persecution of the dragon (interpreted as Satan or the Antichrist).

References: This imagery aligns with the period of protection and sustenance during a time of great tribulation.

Symbolic and Eschatological Significance

Period of Tribulation

1. Persecution of the Saints

Significance: The period of three and a half years is consistently associated with intense tribulation and persecution of God's people. This timeframe is often seen as a period of testing and refining for the faithful.

References: Daniel 7:25 and Revelation 13:5-7 depict this timeframe as one of significant struggle and endurance for the saints.

Divine Protection and Provision

1. God's Sustenance

Significance: Despite the persecution, the period also symbolizes God's protection and provision for His people. The faithful are sustained and preserved even amidst tribulation.

References: Revelation 12:14 emphasizes divine sustenance and protection for the woman in the wilderness.

The Culmination of Prophetic Events

1. Fulfillment of Prophecy

Significance: The period of "time, times, and half a time" signifies the culmination of specific prophetic events, leading to the ultimate fulfillment of God's plan. This period precedes the final resolution and the establishment of God's kingdom.

References: Daniel 12:7 and Revelation 10:7 highlight the completion of prophetic events and the final fulfillment of divine purposes.

Theological Implications

Assurance of God's Sovereignty

1. Divine Control Over History

Significance: The specified period reinforces the assurance of God's sovereignty over history and prophetic events. God determines the duration of tribulation and the ultimate deliverance of His people.

References: Daniel 2:21 - "And He changes the times and the seasons; He removes kings and raises up kings; He gives wisdom to the wise and knowledge to those who have understanding."

Encouragement for Believers

1. Hope Amidst Tribulation

Significance: The prophetic period provides encouragement for believers, assuring them of God's control and ultimate victory despite temporary suffering and persecution.

References: Romans 8:18 - "For I consider that the sufferings of this present time are not worthy to be compared with the glory which shall be revealed in us."

Conclusion

The phrase "time, times, and half a time" in Daniel 12 encapsulates a significant period within the eschatological timeline, symbolizing three and a half years of tribulation, persecution, and divine protection. This period is crucial for understanding the unfolding of prophetic events and the culmination of God's redemptive plan.

By examining its occurrences in both Daniel and Revelation, we gain insight into its symbolic and theological significance, reinforcing the assurance of God's sovereignty and the hope of ultimate deliverance for the faithful. As believers, this understanding encourages us to remain steadfast and hopeful, trusting in God's perfect timing and His ultimate victory over all forces of evil.

CHAPTER 16

THE SYMBOLISM OF NUMBERS IN DANIEL

The Book of Daniel is rich with symbolic imagery, and numbers play a critical role in conveying deeper theological truths and prophetic messages. This chapter will explore the symbolic meanings of key numbers in Daniel, such as seven, seventy, and twelve hundred and ninety days, examining their significance and theological implications within the broader context of biblical numerology.

The Number Seven

Completeness and Perfection

1. Biblical Significance

Explanation: In biblical numerology, the number seven often symbolizes completeness, perfection, and divine order. It appears frequently in both the Old and New

Testaments, underscoring its importance in the divine schema.

References: Genesis 2:2-3 - "And on the seventh day God ended His work which He had done, and He rested on the seventh day from all His work which He had done. Then God blessed the seventh day and sanctified it, because in it He rested from all His work which God had created and made."

Seven Times of Nebuchadnezzar's Madness

Daniel 4:16 - "Let his heart be changed from that of a man, let him be given the heart of a beast, and let seven times pass over him."

1. Symbolic Period of Judgment and Restoration

Interpretation: The "seven times" of Nebuchadnezzar's madness symbolize a complete period of divine judgment and the process of restoration. It reflects the totality of God's plan to humble and then restore the king.

References: Leviticus 26:18 - "And after all this, if you do not obey Me, then I will punish you seven times more for your sins."

The Number Seventy

Completion of a Cycle and Fulfillment

1. Biblical Context

Explanation: The number seventy often signifies the completion of a cycle and the fulfillment of divine purposes. It represents a period of significant duration, often involving judgment, captivity, or deliverance.

References: Jeremiah 29:10 - "For thus says the Lord: After seventy years are completed at Babylon, I will visit you and perform My good word toward you, and cause you to return to this place."

Seventy Weeks Prophecy

Daniel 9:24 - "Seventy weeks are determined for your people and for your holy city, to finish the transgression, to make an end of sins, to make reconciliation for iniquity, to bring in everlasting righteousness, to seal up vision and prophecy, and to anoint the Most Holy."

1. Period of Fulfillment

Interpretation: The "seventy weeks" prophecy represents a divinely appointed period during which God's redemptive plan for Israel and the world is accomplished. This period includes phases of restoration, judgment, and ultimate deliverance.

References: Daniel 9:25-27 details the breakdown of the seventy weeks, indicating specific periods of restoration, the coming of the Messiah, and the final tribulation.

The Number Twelve Hundred and Ninety Days

Time of Tribulation and Waiting

1. Specific Duration

Daniel 12:11 - "And from the time that the daily sacrifice is taken away, and the abomination of desolation is set up, there shall be one thousand two hundred and ninety days."

Explanation: The twelve hundred and ninety days symbolize a specific period of tribulation and waiting, often associated with significant eschatological events. This duration marks the time between a pivotal act of desecration and the fulfillment of divine purposes.

References: Revelation 12:6 - "Then the woman fled into the wilderness, where she has a place prepared by God, that they should feed her there one thousand two hundred and sixty days."

The Number Forty-Five (One Thousand Three Hundred and Thirty-Five Days)

Daniel 12:12 - "Blessed is he who waits, and comes to the one thousand three hundred and thirty-five days."

1. Period of Waiting and Blessing

Explanation: The additional forty-five days beyond the twelve hundred and ninety symbolize a period of waiting that leads to blessing. This extended period emphasizes the importance of perseverance and faithfulness in anticipation of God's ultimate deliverance.

References: The concept of waiting and perseverance is echoed in Revelation 14:12 - "Here is the patience of the saints; here are those who keep the commandments of God and the faith of Jesus."

Theological Implications

Divine Sovereignty and Timing

1. God's Control Over History

Explanation: The specific numbers and durations in Daniel underscore God's sovereignty and precise control over historical and eschatological events. These numbers reflect the unfolding of divine plans according to predetermined timelines.

References: Acts 1:7 - "And He said to them, 'It is not for you to know times or seasons which the Father has put in His own authority.'"

Encouragement for Believers

1. Assurance of Fulfillment

Explanation: The detailed numerical prophecies provide assurance to believers that God's promises will be fulfilled at the appointed times. This certainty encourages faith, perseverance, and hope amidst trials and tribulations.

References: Hebrews 10:23 - "Let us hold fast the confession of our hope without wavering, for He who promised is faithful."

Conclusion

The symbolic use of numbers in the Book of Daniel conveys profound theological truths and reinforces the assurance of divine sovereignty over history. The numbers seven, seventy, twelve hundred and ninety, and one thousand three hundred and thirty-five days all reflect specific periods within God's redemptive plan, emphasizing completeness, fulfillment, tribulation, and waiting.

By understanding the symbolic meanings and theological implications of these numbers, believers can gain deeper insight into God's timing and purposes. This understanding provides encouragement and hope, affirming that God's plans will be accomplished precisely as foretold, leading to the ultimate fulfillment of His kingdom.

CHAPTER 17

THE SOVEREIGNTY OF GOD OVER HISTORY

The Book of Daniel is a profound testament to the sovereignty of God over all aspects of history. Through its rich tapestry of visions and prophecies, Daniel vividly portrays God's supreme control over nations, rulers, and the unfolding of historical events. This chapter will explore the theme of divine sovereignty in Daniel's prophecies, examining how this theme is illustrated through various narratives and prophetic revelations.

God's Sovereignty in the Rise and Fall of Empires

Nebuchadnezzar's Dream of the Statue

Daniel 2:20-21 - "Daniel answered and said: 'Blessed be the name of God forever and ever, for wisdom and might are His. And He changes the times and the seasons; He removes kings and raises up kings; He gives wisdom to the wise and knowledge to those who have understanding.'"

1. The Dream and Its Interpretation

Narrative: King Nebuchadnezzar's dream of a statue composed of various materials (gold, silver, bronze, iron, and clay) represents successive kingdoms, each inferior to the one before it. Daniel interprets the dream, revealing that God has decreed the rise and fall of these empires.

References: Daniel 2:31-45 - The dream's interpretation underscores that God orchestrates the course of history, determining the ascendancy and decline of world powers.

2. The Stone Cut Without Hands

Significance: The stone that destroys the statue and becomes a great mountain symbolizes God's eternal kingdom, which will ultimately prevail over all earthly kingdoms.

References: Daniel 2:44 - "And in the days of these kings the God of heaven will set up a kingdom which shall never be destroyed; and the kingdom shall not be left to other people; it shall break in pieces and consume all these kingdoms, and it shall stand forever."

God's Sovereignty in the Lives of Individuals

The Humbling of Nebuchadnezzar

Daniel 4:34-35 - "And at the end of the time I, Nebuchadnezzar, lifted my eyes to heaven, and my understanding returned to me; and I blessed the Most High and praised and honored Him who lives forever: For His dominion is an everlasting dominion, and His kingdom is from generation to generation. All the inhabitants of the earth are reputed as nothing; He does according to His will in the army of heaven and among the inhabitants of the earth. No one can restrain His hand or say to Him, 'What have You done?'"

1. Nebuchadnezzar's Pride and Fall

Narrative: King Nebuchadnezzar, in his pride, claims credit for the greatness of Babylon. God humbles him, causing him to live as a beast until he acknowledges God's sovereignty.

References: Daniel 4:28-33 - Nebuchadnezzar's period of madness and his eventual restoration highlight God's control over individual destinies and His power to humble the proud.

2. The King's Acknowledgment of God's Sovereignty

Significance: Nebuchadnezzar's restoration and his proclamation of God's sovereignty serve as a powerful testament to God's authority over human rulers and His ability to change hearts.

References: Daniel 4:37 - "Now I, Nebuchadnezzar, praise and extol and honor the King of heaven, all of whose works are truth, and His ways justice. And those who walk in pride He is able to put down."

God's Sovereignty in Prophetic Revelation

The Vision of the Four Beasts

Daniel 7:13-14 - "I was watching in the night visions, and behold, One like the Son of Man, coming with the clouds of heaven! He came to the Ancient of Days, and they brought Him near before Him. Then to Him was given dominion and glory and a kingdom, that all peoples, nations, and languages should serve Him. His dominion is an everlasting dominion, which shall not pass away, and His kingdom the one which shall not be destroyed."

1. The Four Beasts and the Ancient of Days

Narrative: Daniel's vision of the four beasts emerging from the sea represents successive empires. The Ancient of Days, symbolizing God, presides over a divine court that ultimately judges and destroys these beasts.

References: Daniel 7:1-12 - The vision underscores God's judgment and authority over the empires of the world.

2. The Everlasting Kingdom

Significance: The vision culminates in the presentation of an everlasting kingdom to the "Son of Man," who is given authority over all nations. This signifies the ultimate establishment of God's eternal rule.

References: Daniel 7:27 - "Then the kingdom and dominion, and the greatness of the kingdoms under the whole heaven, shall be given to the people, the saints of the Most High. His kingdom is an everlasting kingdom, and all dominions shall serve and obey Him."

God's Sovereignty in Deliverance and Judgment

The Fiery Furnace and the Lion's Den

Daniel 3:17-18 - "If that is the case, our God whom we serve is able to deliver us from the burning fiery furnace, and He will deliver us from your hand, O king. But if not, let it be known to you, O king, that we do not serve your gods, nor will we worship the gold image which you have set up."

1. The Fiery Furnace

Narrative: Shadrach, Meshach, and Abednego refuse to worship Nebuchadnezzar's golden image and are thrown into a fiery furnace. God miraculously delivers them, demonstrating His power over life and death.

References: Daniel 3:19-27 - Their deliverance serves as a testament to God's ability to protect His faithful servants and His sovereignty over all earthly powers.

Daniel 6:22 - "My God sent His angel and shut the lions' mouths so that they have not hurt me, because I was found innocent before Him; and also, O king, I have done no wrong before you."

2. The Lion's Den

Narrative: Daniel's faithfulness to God leads to his being thrown into a lion's den by King Darius. God delivers Daniel by shutting the mouths of the lions, demonstrating His sovereignty and power to save.

References: Daniel 6:19-23 - Daniel's miraculous preservation underscores God's authority and His ability to deliver His people from seemingly impossible situations.

God's Sovereignty in Eschatological Fulfillment

The Seventy Weeks Prophecy

Daniel 9:24 - "Seventy weeks are determined for your people and for your holy city, to finish the transgression, to make an end of sins, to make reconciliation for iniquity, to bring in everlasting righteousness, to seal up vision and prophecy, and to anoint the Most Holy."

1. The Prophetic Timeline

Explanation: The seventy weeks prophecy outlines God's sovereign timeline for bringing about the redemption and ultimate restoration of Israel. This period encompasses the coming of the Messiah, the atonement for sin, and the establishment of everlasting righteousness.

References: Daniel 9:25-27 - The detailed breakdown of the seventy weeks highlights God's meticulous planning and control over historical and eschatological events.

Theological Implications

Assurance of Divine Control

1. Comfort in Uncertainty

Explanation: The theme of God's sovereignty in Daniel provides comfort and assurance to believers that, despite the chaos and uncertainties of history, God remains in control and His purposes will ultimately prevail.

References: Isaiah 46:9-10 - "Remember the former things of old, for I am God, and there is no other; I am God, and there is none like Me, declaring the end from the beginning, and from ancient times things that are not yet done, saying, 'My counsel shall stand, and I will do all My pleasure.'"

Encouragement for Faithfulness

1. Call to Trust and Obedience

Explanation: Understanding God's sovereignty encourages believers to remain faithful and obedient, trusting in His ultimate plan and deliverance, even in the face of trials and persecution.

References: Romans 8:28 - "And we know that all things work together for good to those who love God, to those who are the called according to His purpose."

Conclusion

The sovereignty of God over history is a central theme in the Book of Daniel, vividly illustrated through the rise and fall of empires, the lives of individuals, prophetic revelations, and divine deliverance. Daniel's visions and prophecies affirm that God is in ultimate control of all historical and eschatological events, orchestrating them according to His divine plan.

For believers, this assurance of God's sovereignty provides comfort, encouragement, and a call to remain faithful. It reminds us that, regardless of the uncertainties and challenges we face, God's purposes will prevail, and His kingdom will be established forever. As we reflect on Daniel's prophecies, we are invited to deepen our trust in God's sovereign rule and look forward with hope to the fulfillment of His redemptive plan.

The Kingdom of God versus the Kingdoms of the World

The Book of Daniel presents a profound contrast between the Kingdom of God and the kingdoms of the world. Through visions, dreams, and prophetic revelations, Daniel illustrates the transient nature of earthly powers and the enduring sovereignty of God's kingdom. This chapter will explore the distinct characteristics of the Kingdom of God and the kingdoms of the world, examining their interactions and the ultimate triumph of God's eternal dominion.

The Kingdoms of the World

The Dream of Nebuchadnezzar's Statue

Daniel 2:31-35 - "You, O king, were watching; and behold, a great image! This great image, whose splendor was excellent, stood before you; and its form was awesome. This image's head was of fine gold, its chest, and arms of silver, its belly and thighs of bronze, its legs of iron, its feet partly of iron and partly of clay. You watched while a stone was cut out without hands, which struck the image on its feet of iron and clay, and broke them in pieces."

1. The Composition of the Statue

Description: The statue in Nebuchadnezzar's dream is composed of various materials, each representing a different kingdom. The head of gold symbolizes Babylon, the chest and arms of silver represent the Medo-Persian Empire, the belly and thighs of bronze signify Greece, and the legs of iron and feet of iron and clay denote Rome and its fragmented successors.

References: Daniel 2:36-43 - Daniel interprets the dream, explaining the succession of these empires and their eventual downfall.

2. The Fragility and Transience of Earthly Kingdoms

Interpretation: The varying materials illustrate the diminishing strength and increasing fragility of successive empires. The feet of iron mixed with clay highlight the inherent instability and ultimate vulnerability of human political structures.

References: Daniel 2:42-43 - "And as the toes of the feet were partly of iron and partly of clay, so the kingdom shall be partly strong and partly fragile. As you saw iron mixed with ceramic clay, they will mingle with the seed of men; but they will not adhere to one another, just as iron does not mix with clay."

The Kingdom of God

The Stone Cut Without Hands

Daniel 2:44-45 - "And in the days of these kings the God of heaven will set up a kingdom which shall never be destroyed, and the kingdom shall not be left to other people; it shall break in pieces and consume all these kingdoms, and it shall stand forever. Since you saw that the stone was cut out of the mountain without hands and that it broke in pieces the iron, the bronze, the clay, the silver, and the gold—the great

God has made known to the king what will come to pass after this. The dream is certain, and its interpretation is sure."

1. The Divine Origin and Eternal Nature

Description: The stone "cut out without hands" symbolizes the Kingdom of God, characterized by its divine origin and eternal nature. Unlike the transient and fragile earthly kingdoms, God's kingdom is indestructible and everlasting.

References: Psalm 145:13 - "Your kingdom is an everlasting kingdom, and Your dominion endures throughout all generations."

2. The Supremacy of God's Kingdom

Interpretation: The stone's destruction of the statue signifies the ultimate triumph of God's kingdom over all earthly powers. This act illustrates the comprehensive and final victory of divine sovereignty over human political systems.

References: Revelation 11:15 - "Then the seventh angel sounded: And there were loud voices in heaven, saying, 'The kingdoms of this world have become the kingdoms of our Lord and of His Christ, and He shall reign forever and ever!'"

The Conflict Between the Kingdoms

The Vision of the Four Beasts

Daniel 7:2-3 - "Daniel spoke, saying, 'I saw in my vision by night, and behold, the four winds of heaven were stirring up the Great Sea. And four great beasts came up from the sea, each different from the other.'"

1. Symbolism of the Beasts

Description: The four beasts emerging from the sea represent successive world empires, each characterized by violence, chaos, and opposition to God's purposes. These beasts symbolize the destructive and oppressive nature of worldly kingdoms.

References: Daniel 7:17 - "Those great beasts, which are four, are four kings which arise out of the earth."

2. The Divine Judgment and Victory

Interpretation: The vision culminates with the judgment of the beasts by the Ancient of Days and the establishment of the Son of Man's eternal kingdom. This sequence underscores the inevitability of divine justice and the ultimate defeat of earthly powers.

References: Daniel 7:26-27 - "But the court shall be seated, and they shall take away his dominion, to consume and destroy it forever. Then the kingdom and dominion, and the greatness of the kingdoms under the whole heaven, shall be given to the people, the saints of the Most High. His kingdom is an everlasting kingdom, and all dominions shall serve and obey Him."

Characteristics of the Kingdom of God

Righteousness and Justice

1. The Nature of God's Rule

Description: The Kingdom of God is characterized by righteousness, justice, and peace. Unlike the corrupt and oppressive rule of earthly kingdoms, God's reign is marked by fairness and moral integrity.

References: Isaiah 9:7 - "Of the increase of His government and peace there will be no end, upon the throne of David and over His kingdom, to order it and establish it with judgment and justice from that time forward, even forever. The zeal of the Lord of hosts will perform this."

Inclusivity and Universality

1. The Scope of God's Kingdom

Description: God's kingdom is inclusive and universal, transcending national and ethnic boundaries. It encompasses people from all nations, tribes, and languages, reflecting the global scope of God's redemptive plan.

References: Revelation 7:9 - "After these things I looked, and behold, a great multitude which no one could number, of all nations, tribes, peoples, and tongues, standing before the throne and before the Lamb, clothed with white robes, with palm branches in their hands."

Eternality and Stability

1. The Unshakeable Nature

Description: Unlike the kingdoms of the world, which are temporary and prone to instability, God's kingdom is eternal and unshakeable. It stands forever, unaltered by the passage of time or the rise and fall of human powers.

References: Hebrews 12:28 - "Therefore, since we are receiving a kingdom which cannot be shaken, let us have grace, by which we may serve God acceptably with reverence and godly fear."

The Ultimate Triumph of God's Kingdom

The Vision of the Ram and the Goat

Daniel 8:20-22 - "The ram which you saw, having the two horns—they are the kings of Media and Persia. And the male goat is the kingdom of Greece. The large horn that is between its eyes is the first king. As for the broken horn and the four that stood up in its place, four kingdoms shall arise out of that nation, but not with its power."

1. The Rise and Fall of Empires

Description: The vision of the ram and the goat highlights the rise and fall of the Medo-Persian and Greek empires, respectively. This vision reinforces the transient nature of earthly powers and the ultimate sovereignty of God.

References: Daniel 8:25 - "Through his cunning, he shall cause deceit to prosper under his rule; and he shall exalt himself in his heart. He shall destroy many in their prosperity. He shall even rise against the Prince of princes, but he shall be broken without human means."

The Eternal Dominion of the Son of Man

Daniel 7:13-14 - "I was watching in the night visions, and behold, One like the Son of Man, coming with the clouds of heaven! He came to the Ancient of Days, and they brought Him near before Him. Then to Him was given dominion and glory and a kingdom, that all peoples, nations, and languages should serve Him. His dominion is an everlasting dominion, which shall not pass away, and His kingdom the one which shall not be destroyed."

1. The Son of Man's Reign

Description: The vision of the Son of Man receiving an eternal kingdom from the Ancient of Days symbolizes the ultimate establishment of God's rule. This eternal dominion is characterized by justice, peace, and the worship of all peoples.

References: Matthew 24:30 - "Then the sign of the Son of Man will appear in heaven, and then all the tribes of the earth will mourn, and they will see the Son of Man coming on the clouds of heaven with power and great glory."

Theological Implications

The Assurance of God's Sovereignty

1. Trust in Divine Rule

Explanation: The contrast between the Kingdom of God and the kingdoms of the world provides assurance of God's ultimate sovereignty and control over history. Believers are encouraged to trust in God's eternal plan and His righteous rule.

References: Psalm 103:19 - "The Lord has established His throne in heaven, and His kingdom rules over all."

The Call to Faithfulness and Hope

1. Encouragement for Believers

Explanation: The certainty of God's kingdom encourages believers to remain faithful and hopeful, even in the face of worldly challenges and injustices. It assures them of the eventual triumph of God's purposes.

References: 1 Corinthians 15:24-

25 - "Then comes the end, when He delivers the kingdom to God the Father, when He puts an end to all rule and all authority and power. For He must reign till He has put all enemies under His feet."

Conclusion

The Book of Daniel powerfully contrasts the Kingdom of God with the kingdoms of the world, highlighting the transient and fragile nature of earthly powers and the eternal, righteous reign of God. Through visions, dreams, and prophetic revelations, Daniel underscores the ultimate sovereignty of God and the inevitable triumph of His kingdom.

For believers, this contrast provides assurance, encouragement, and a call to remain faithful. It reminds us that despite the rise and fall of human empires, God's kingdom endures forever, offering hope and stability in a world of uncertainty. As we reflect on Daniel's prophecies, we are invited to align our lives with the values of God's kingdom and look forward with hope to the fulfillment of His eternal reign.

The Role of Israel in God's Redemptive Plan

The Book of Daniel, along with other biblical texts, highlights the central role of Israel in God's redemptive plan. Israel's history, prophecies, and covenant relationship with God serve as a testament to God's ongoing work in the world. This chapter will explore the unique role of Israel in the unfolding of God's salvation history, examining its past, present, and future significance within the framework of biblical prophecy and theology.

The Covenant Relationship

The Abrahamic Covenant

Genesis 12:1-3 - "Now the Lord had said to Abram: 'Get out of your country, from your family and from your father's house, to a land that I will show you. I will make you a great nation; I will bless you and make your name great; and you shall be a blessing. I will bless those who bless you, and I will curse him who curses you, and in you, all the families of the earth shall be blessed.'"

1. The Promise to Abraham

Description: The Abrahamic Covenant marks the beginning of Israel's unique role in God's redemptive plan. God promises to make Abraham a great nation, bless him, and through him, bless all the families of the earth.

References: Genesis 17:4-8 - God reaffirms the covenant with Abraham, promising to establish an everlasting covenant with him and his descendants.

The Mosaic Covenant

Exodus 19:5-6 - "Now therefore, if you will indeed obey My voice and keep My covenant, then you shall be a special treasure to Me above all people; for all the earth is Mine. And you shall be to Me a kingdom of priests and a holy nation. These are the words which you shall speak to the children of Israel."

1. The Giving of the Law

Description: The Mosaic Covenant establishes Israel as a kingdom of priests and a holy nation. Through the Law given at Sinai, Israel is called to live in a way that reflects God's holiness and justice.

References: Deuteronomy 7:6 - "For you are a holy people to the Lord your God; the Lord your God has chosen you to be a people for Himself, a special treasure above all the peoples on the face of the earth."

Israel in Prophecy

The Babylonian Exile and Restoration

Daniel 9:2 - "In the first year of his reign I, Daniel, understood by the books the number of the years specified by the word of the Lord through Jeremiah the prophet, that He would accomplish seventy years in the desolations of Jerusalem."

1. Exile and Hope of Restoration

Description: The Babylonian exile serves as both a judgment for Israel's unfaithfulness and a period of purification. The prophecies of restoration emphasize God's commitment to His covenant people and His plan to bring them back to their land.

References: Jeremiah 29:10-11 - "For thus says the Lord: After seventy years are completed at Babylon, I will visit you and perform My good word toward you, and cause you to return to this place. For I know the thoughts that I think toward you, says the Lord, thoughts of peace and not of evil, to give you a future and a hope."

The Seventy Weeks Prophecy

Daniel 9:24-27 - "Seventy weeks are determined for your people and for your holy city, to finish the transgression, to make an end of sins, to make reconciliation for iniquity, to bring in everlasting righteousness, to seal up vision and prophecy, and to anoint the Most Holy."

1. Fulfillment and Future Hope

Description: The prophecy of the seventy weeks outlines God's redemptive plan for Israel, culminating in the coming of the Messiah and the ultimate establishment of His kingdom. This period includes phases of restoration, judgment, and final deliverance.

References: Daniel 9:25-26 - The prophecy details the coming of an Anointed One and the subsequent events that lead to the final fulfillment of God's promises to Israel.

Israel and the Messiah

The First Coming of Christ

Isaiah 53:5-6 - "But He was wounded for our transgressions, He was bruised for our iniquities; the chastisement for our peace was upon Him, and by His stripes we are healed. All we like sheep have gone astray; we have turned, everyone, to his own way; and the Lord has laid on Him the iniquity of us all."

1. The Suffering Servant

Description: The prophecies concerning the Messiah emphasize His role as the Suffering Servant who bears the sins of many. Jesus Christ's first coming fulfills these prophecies, providing redemption for Israel and the world.

References: Matthew 1:21 - "And she will bring forth a Son, and you shall call His name Jesus, for He will save His people from their sins."

The Role of Israel in the Early Church

Romans 1:16 - "For I am not ashamed of the gospel of Christ, for it is the power of God to salvation for everyone who believes, for the Jew first and also for the Greek."

1. The Gospel to the Jew First

Description: The early church's mission reflects the priority of reaching the Jewish people with the gospel. Israel's role is pivotal in the initial spread of Christianity and the establishment of the early church.

References: Acts 1:8 - "But you shall receive power when the Holy Spirit has come upon you, and you shall be witnesses to Me in Jerusalem, and in all Judea and Samaria, and to the end of the earth."

Israel's Future in Prophecy

The Restoration of Israel

Romans 11:25-26 - "For I do not desire, brethren, that you should be ignorant of this mystery, lest you should be wise in your own opinion, that blindness in part has happened to Israel until the fullness of the Gentiles has come in. And so all Israel will be saved, as it is written: 'The Deliverer will come out of Zion, and He will turn away ungodliness from Jacob.'"

1. The Fullness of Israel's Salvation

Description: Paul's writings in Romans emphasize the future restoration and salvation of Israel. God's covenant promises to Israel remain intact, and their fulfillment includes a future turning of the Jewish people to the Messiah.

References: Romans 11:29 - "For the gifts and the calling of God are irrevocable."

The Role in the Millennial Kingdom

Revelation 20:4-6 - "And I saw thrones, and they sat on them, and judgment was committed to them. Then I saw the souls of those who had been beheaded for their witness to Jesus and for the word of God, who had not worshiped the beast or his image and had not received his mark on their foreheads or on their hands. And they lived and reigned with Christ for a thousand years."

1. Israel's Reign with Christ

Description: In the Millennial Kingdom, Israel will play a significant role, reigning with Christ and experiencing the fulfillment of God's promises. This period of peace and justice will showcase the ultimate restoration of Israel.

References: Isaiah 2:2-3 - "Now it shall come to pass in the latter days that the mountain of the Lord's house shall be established on the top of the mountains, and shall be exalted above the hills; and all nations shall flow to it. Many people shall come and say, 'Come, and let us go up to the mountain of the Lord, to the house of the God of Jacob; He will teach us His ways, and we shall walk in His paths.' For out of Zion shall go forth the law, and the word of the Lord from Jerusalem."

Theological Implications

God's Faithfulness to His Promises

1. Assurance of Covenant Faithfulness

Explanation: The consistent role of Israel in God's redemptive plan underscores His faithfulness to His covenant promises. Despite Israel's unfaithfulness, God remains committed to fulfilling His word.

References: Deuteronomy 7:9 - "Therefore know that the Lord your God, He is God, the faithful God who keeps covenant and mercy for a thousand generations with those who love Him and keep His commandments."

The Inclusion of the Gentiles

1. Universal Scope of Salvation

Explanation: While Israel holds a unique place in God's plan, the inclusion of the Gentiles demonstrates the universal scope of God's salvation. The church, composed of both Jews and Gentiles, reflects God's redemptive purposes for all humanity.

References: Ephesians 2:14-16 - "For He Himself is our peace, who has made both one, and has broken down the middle wall of separation, having abolished in His flesh the enmity, that is, the law of commandments contained in ordinances, so as to create in Himself one new man from the two, thus making peace, and that He might reconcile them both to God in one body through the cross, thereby putting to death the enmity."

Conclusion

The role of Israel in God's redemptive plan is a central theme throughout the Bible, prominently highlighted in the Book of Daniel. From the covenant promises to Abraham and Moses to the prophecies of restoration and the coming of the Messiah, Israel's journey reflects God's unchanging faithfulness and sovereign plan.

As we look forward to the future fulfillment of God's promises, Israel's story continues to provide hope and assurance of God's covenant faithfulness. The inclusion of the Gentiles in this redemptive plan broadens the scope of God's salvation, demonstrating His love and mercy for all humanity. Ultimately, Israel's role in God's redemptive plan serves as a powerful testament to the unfolding of divine purposes and the certainty of God's promises.

CHAPTER 18

INTERPRETING DANIEL'S SYMBOLS IN CONTEMPORARY TIME

The Book of Daniel, with its rich tapestry of prophetic symbols and visions, has long captivated the minds of believers and scholars alike. While these symbols had immediate relevance to the historical context in which Daniel wrote, they also possess timeless significance that extends to contemporary world events. This chapter explores how Daniel's prophetic symbols can be interpreted today, offering insights and lessons for modern-day believers navigating a complex and often tumultuous world.

The Four Beasts and Modern Empires

The Symbolism of the Four Beasts

Daniel 7:2-3 - "Daniel spoke, saying, 'I saw in my vision by night, and behold, the four winds of heaven were stirring up the Great Sea. And four great beasts came up from the sea, each different from the other.'"

1. The Lion with Eagle's Wings

Interpretation: Traditionally seen as representing Babylon, the lion with an eagle's wings can symbolize a powerful and majestic empire that eventually loses its swiftness and strength.

Contemporary Application: This symbol can be seen in modern superpowers whose influence and power are unmatched but are also vulnerable to internal decay and external challenges.

2. The Bear Raised on One Side

Interpretation: Representing the Medo-Persian Empire, the bear signifies strength and aggression, with an uneven balance of power.

Contemporary Application: This could be applied to modern nations or coalitions that exhibit military strength and strategic dominance but are plagued by internal imbalances and inequities.

3. The Leopard with Four Wings and Four Heads

Interpretation: Symbolizing the Greek Empire under Alexander the Great, the leopard represents swiftness, division, and multiplicity of leadership.

Contemporary Application: This can reflect modern states or multinational corporations characterized by rapid expansion, innovation, and complex leadership structures.

4. The Dreadful and Terrible Beast

Interpretation: Often associated with the Roman Empire, this beast symbolizes unparalleled power, brutality, and the capacity to crush and devour.

Contemporary Application: This could represent authoritarian regimes or global institutions that wield immense power and influence, often at the cost of oppression and exploitation.

The Statue in Nebuchadnezzar's Dream

The Decline of World Powers

Daniel 2:31-45 - "You, O king, were watching; and behold, a great image! This great image, whose splendor was excellent, stood before you; and its form was awesome. This image's head was of fine gold, its chest, and arms of silver, its belly and thighs of bronze, its legs of iron, its feet partly of iron and partly of clay."

1. The Head of Gold

Interpretation: Representing Babylon, the head of gold symbolizes supreme power and wealth.

Contemporary Application: This can be likened to modern economic superpowers whose wealth and influence dominate the global stage.

2. The Chest and Arms of Silver

Interpretation: Symbolizing the Medo-Persian Empire, the silver represents a significant but lesser degree of power compared to gold.

Contemporary Application: This could represent nations or regions that hold substantial but not absolute global influence.

3. The Belly and Thighs of Bronze

Interpretation: Representing the Greek Empire, bronze symbolizes a strong but divided power.

Contemporary Application: Modern federations or alliances that are strong yet divided by internal politics and cultural differences can be seen in this light.

4. The Legs of Iron and Feet of Iron and Clay

Interpretation: Representing the Roman Empire, iron signifies strength, while the mixture with clay indicates inherent weakness and instability.

Contemporary Application: This can be seen in modern political entities or unions that possess great power but are fundamentally unstable and prone to fragmentation.

5. The Stone Cut Without Hands

Interpretation: Symbolizing the Kingdom of God, the stone represents a divine intervention that destroys the earthly kingdoms and establishes an eternal dominion.

Contemporary Application: This underscores the ultimate sovereignty of God over all human affairs and the eventual triumph of His kingdom over worldly powers.

The Seventy Weeks Prophecy

Understanding Modern Prophetic Timelines

Daniel 9:24-27 - "Seventy weeks are determined for your people and for your holy city, to finish the transgression, to make an end of sins, to make reconciliation for iniquity, to bring in everlasting righteousness, to seal up vision and prophecy, and to anoint the Most Holy."

1. The Period of Seventy Weeks

Interpretation: Traditionally interpreted as 490 years, culminating in significant events such as the coming of the Messiah and subsequent tribulations.

Contemporary Application: This can be seen as a framework for understanding the unfolding of significant historical and eschatological events, prompting believers to remain vigilant and discerning of the times.

2. The Anointed One and the Covenant

Interpretation: The prophecy points to the coming of the Messiah and the establishment of a new covenant.

Contemporary Application: This highlights the ongoing relevance of Christ's redemptive work and the importance of living in the reality of the new covenant amidst contemporary challenges.

The Role of Israel and Global Dynamics

Israel in Modern Prophecy

Daniel 12:1 - "At that time Michael shall stand up, the great prince who stands watch over the sons of your people; and there shall be a time of trouble, such as never was since there was a nation, even to that time. And at that time your people shall be delivered, everyone who is found written in the book."

1. Israel's Enduring Significance

Interpretation: Israel's role in prophetic events highlights its central place in God's redemptive plan.

Contemporary Application: The modern state of Israel and its geopolitical dynamics can be viewed through the lens of biblical prophecy, encouraging believers to pray for peace and understand the broader implications of Israel's destiny.

2. Global Implications

Interpretation: The events surrounding Israel often have global repercussions, indicating the interconnectedness of prophetic and geopolitical realities.

Contemporary Application: This underscores the importance of understanding global events in light of biblical prophecy and seeking to discern God's purposes in contemporary world affairs.

Living Out the Lessons of Daniel's Prophecies

Faithfulness and Wisdom

Daniel 12:3 - "Those who are wise shall shine like the brightness of the firmament, and those who turn many to righteousness like the stars forever and ever."

1. The Call to Wisdom

Interpretation: The prophecies call for a response of wisdom and faithfulness from God's people.

Contemporary Application: Believers are called to live wisely and faithfully, turning many to righteousness and reflecting the light of Christ in a complex world.

2. The Assurance of God's Sovereignty

Interpretation: The overarching theme of Daniel's prophecies is the sovereignty of God over history and human affairs.

Contemporary Application: This provides assurance and hope, encouraging believers to trust in God's ultimate control and to live with confidence in His promises.

Conclusion

Interpreting Daniel's symbols in the context of contemporary world events offers profound insights and lessons for modern-day believers. The themes of God's sovereignty, the transient nature of earthly powers, the enduring significance of Israel, and the call to wisdom and faithfulness resonate deeply in today's complex and often tumultuous world.

By understanding the relevance of Daniel's prophecies, believers can navigate contemporary challenges with a biblical perspective, living out their faith with hope, discernment, and a steadfast commitment to God's eternal kingdom. As we reflect on these timeless truths, we are reminded that, despite the uncertainties and upheavals of our times, God's sovereign plan is unfolding, and His purposes will ultimately prevail.

CONCLUSION

The Book of Daniel stands as a remarkable testament to the power of prophetic revelation and the sovereignty of God over history. Through its vivid imagery, detailed prophecies, and profound theological themes, Daniel provides a treasure trove of insights that continue to inspire and challenge believers today. As we have explored the symbolic meanings of Daniel's visions and dreams, we have uncovered layers of understanding that reveal God's unfolding plan for humanity and the ultimate triumph of His kingdom.

The Importance of Prophetic Symbols

Prophetic symbols serve as a bridge between the divine and the human, allowing us to glimpse the larger narrative of God's redemptive plan. In Daniel, these symbols convey deep truths about the rise and fall of empires, the nature of divine judgment, and the promise of ultimate restoration. By engaging with these symbols, we gain a richer understanding of how God interacts with the world and how His purposes are realized through the course of history.

Key Themes and Lessons

The Sovereignty of God

One of the central themes of Daniel is the absolute sovereignty of God over all earthly powers. The visions of the four beasts, the statue in Nebuchadnezzar's dream, and the various prophetic timelines all emphasize that God is in control, orchestrating the events of history according to His divine will. This assurance of God's sovereignty provides comfort and hope, especially in times of uncertainty and turmoil.

The Role of Israel

Daniel highlights the unique role of Israel in God's redemptive plan. From the covenant promises to the prophetic visions of restoration and the coming of the Messiah, Israel's journey reflects God's faithfulness and His commitment to His chosen people. Understanding Israel's role helps us appreciate the continuity of God's plan and the inclusion of all nations in His redemptive purposes.

The Kingdom of God vs. the Kingdoms of the World

The contrast between the Kingdom of God and the kingdoms of the world is vividly depicted in Daniel. While earthly kingdoms rise and fall, characterized by power, corruption, and eventual decline, the Kingdom of God is eternal, just, and unshakeable. This contrast invites believers to place their trust in God's eternal kingdom rather than in the transient powers of this world.

Contemporary Relevance

The prophetic symbols in Daniel are not confined to ancient history; they resonate deeply with contemporary world events. As we navigate a complex and often tumultuous world, the lessons from Daniel offer guidance and perspective. The visions and prophecies encourage us to remain faithful, wise, and hopeful, trusting in God's ultimate plan and His righteous rule.

Encouragement for Believers

This book aims to provide a comprehensive guide to the prophetic symbols in Daniel, encouraging readers to delve deeper into the mysteries of this remarkable biblical text. By understanding these symbols, we can draw closer to God, gain insight into His unfolding plan, and live with greater confidence in His promises.

Final Reflections

The journey through Daniel's prophecies is both challenging and enriching. It calls us to engage with the text at a deeper level, to seek understanding through prayer and study, and to apply its lessons to our lives. As we reflect on the profound themes and vivid symbols of Daniel, we are reminded that God's plans are perfect, His timing is impeccable, and His kingdom will ultimately triumph over all.

In conclusion, the Book of Daniel offers a timeless message of hope, sovereignty, and divine purpose. May this exploration of its prophetic symbols inspire and equip believers to live with faith and conviction, anticipating the glorious fulfillment of God's redemptive plan for humanity.

www.ingramcontent.com/pod-product-compliance
Lightning Source LLC
Chambersburg PA
CBHW061244120726
48001CB00001B/137